Cruise Through the Blues

Cruise Through the Blues

Barry Hansen

Foreword by B.B. King

Miller Freeman Books

SAN FRANCISCO

Published by Miller Freeman Books
600 Harrison Street, San Francisco, CA 94107
An imprint of Miller Freeman, Inc.
Publishers of Guitar Player, Bass Player and Keyboard magazines
The Music Player Network
www.musicplayer.com

Distributed to the book trade in the U.S. and Canada by
Publishers Group West, 1700 Fourth Street, Berkeley, CA 94710

Distributed to the music trade in the U.S. and Canada by
Hal Leonard Corp., P.O. Box 13819, Milwaukee, WI 53213

Editor: Harold Bronson / Steve Baeck
Art Director: Chitra Sekhar
Production Artist: Bill Neary
Cover Design and Interior Typesetting: Brad Greene
Front Cover photos: Muddy Waters (courtesy of Jas Obrecht);
   detail of Blind John Davis (Frank Driggs Collection/Archive
   Photos); Magic Sam (courtesy of Delmark Records); Charlie
   Musselwhite (courtesy of Vanguard Records); Stevie Ray
   Vaughan (courtesy of Sony)

Library of Congress Cataloging-in-Publication Data
   Hansen, Barry, 1941–
      Rhino's cruise through the blues / by Barry Hansen;
      foreword by B.B. King
         p.   cm.
      "Discographical Note": p.
      ISBN 0-87930-625-4
         1. Blues (Music)—History and criticism. 2. Blues
      musicians I. Title.

   ML3521.H37 2000   98-004240
   781.643'09—dc21

Printed in the United States of America

00 01 02 03 04 05   5 4 3 2 1

Table of Contents

Dedication

To my parents, lovers of books and music…to D. K. Wilgus, Ed Pearl, Bernie Pearl, Dave Cohen, Mark Naftalin, Mike Bloomfield, Bob Hite, Alan Wilson, and Art Rupe, who showed me the ways…to all the singers and players in this book…Rebecca Davis, for sharing her research on Alan Wilson… Harold Bronson, James Austin and everyone at Rhino and Miller Freeman…Steve Baeck…and especially my wife, Sue.

FOREWORD BY B.B. KING

I came to the blues in a roundabout way. I started out wanting to be a gospel singer; I wanted to play guitar in the sanctified church, like our pastor. At that time, I was a tractor driver on a plantation in the Delta. But on weekends, when I'd get off work, I would go to nearby towns and sit on the street corner and play.

People who would request a gospel song would always compliment me very politely, pat me on the head and say, "Son, if you keep that up you're gonna be great some day." But they never tipped. People who would request the blues would always put a tip in my hat, and sometimes buy me a beer. On the plantation, I was making the top salary for that kind of work: twenty-two-and-a-half dollars, working a six-and-a-half day week. On evenings, just sittin' on street corners, I would sometimes make fifty to sixty dollars. So, I quit the plantation and became a blues singer full time.

I was originally inspired by Lonnie Johnson—an acoustic guitarist who sang blues. He also worked with Louis Armstrong, Duke Ellington, Bessie Smith and Mahalia Jackson, which made him very unique, and I wanted to be like him. Blind Lemon Jefferson, a Texas blues singer, was another acoustic guitarist who was an influence. I had a cousin, Bukka White, whose playing I liked, but whose influence went past music. He explained to me the importance of being polite. He said to act like you're going to borrow money, and to talk as if you're dating the preacher's daughter.

I remember when I heard T-Bone Walker playing single-string blues on the electric guitar. That's when I went crazy for the guitar, and I've been crazy ever since. I also loved the playing of jazz guitarists Django Reinhardt and Charlie Christian. Charlie was one of the first blacks to work in a white band; he worked with Benny Goodman's sextet. There are so many singers and players, not only of the guitar, who influenced me; I am a mixture of many.

Blues to me is very much more than the music. I have always found it very educational. It has been a way of life, because it's all about our feelings about the people, places, and things we've known. The blues started with the slaves and their disciples and led on into me; now I'm one of the disciples. Even so, while most people only think of the sad, painful parts of the blues, I find a lot of joy in it.

When I started playing the blues, my subject matter was the people near me. When I moved to the city, I could sing about that, too. Now that I travel the world, everything that has to do with pleasure, joy, and sadness around the world concerns me and influences my music. I think that plays a big part in the blues with everybody; that's why the blues lives on today. I've played blues clubs from Japan to Russia, and I've seen a lot of young people in the audience. The young people are playing the blues today, they're supporting it today, and it's popular all over the world. That's because everyone can relate to the simplicity and honesty of the blues. There's nothing like it.

INTRODUCTION: THE KING, AND A PRINCE

Blues has been around for a hundred years or so…and yet in many ways it's bigger than ever today. Not many other forms of music can make that statement.

As blues begins its second century, you can hear live blues regularly in any good-sized American city (and some not so good-sized—not to mention hundreds of cities around the world—Osaka, Japan has a very lively blues scene, for instance). You can see and hear blues frequently on TV and radio. You can find good blues in practically any "record" store, anywhere in the U.S.A. (and, again, around the world). None of this was true in 1927, 1937, 1947, 1957 or any other "golden year" you might name.

Pretty good for a brand of music that was all but dead and buried not too long ago.

◆

What keeps this old music so young? Why do so many people enjoy it so much nowadays? Blues is user-friendly, for one thing. You don't have to go to school to learn how it works. It comes from the heart, not from a microchip.

Blues is comfort music. Though it's changed through the years, many things about it have always remained the same. Old songs, old licks and old feelings shine through in today's blues, moving the mind, soul and body with the delight of recognition.

Most of all, blues is the ultimate feel-good music. Whatever mood you may be in, you'll be in a better one after you hear some good blues.

That's what blues was created for, after all. Blues was developed by and for people who very badly needed something to make them feel better…people who did back-breaking labor for starvation wages, and were abused and tyrannized from here to Clarksdale…people who lived with hardly more freedom and sustenance than their parents had when they were slaves not all that long before.

With all that, it's somehow miraculous that blues speaks so powerfully and enjoyably to so many people today…even people who never ate chitlin's, have never been anywhere near Clarksdale, and struck it rich in software at 19. Blues is miraculous music.

Blues isn't all alike, of course. There have been a lot of different kinds of blues through the years. The way all of them have evolved and interacted with each other is fascinating, and we'll explore those pathways in these pages.

Naturally, most blues fans will come to like certain styles more than others…but as a group, blues fans are remarkable for the way they love and respect all good blues, old or new. Go to a blues festival and you're likely to hear quite a mixture of styles…with some gospel in there too for good measure, especially if it's Sunday. Quite a contrast to today's rock/pop scene.

◆

Let's start right at the top, with **B. B. King** (born Riley B. King, 1925)—by popular and critical acclaim, the King of Blues. He started out in the 1940s, became a star in the 1950s, then kept the faith through some leaner years. When new generations discovered blues in the 1980s and 1990s, B.B. was there to welcome them.

It's not surprising that so many other performers today have at least a little B.B. in their style. Meanwhile the man himself keeps opening new doors for blues. A charismatic yet dignified performer, a good citizen, and a man who takes care of business, B.B. has buried once and for all the old stereotype of the bluesman as a drunken, self-destructive rogue.

B.B. was born in rural Mississippi, which has produced more blues artists per capita than any other state, and can make a fair claim to being the place where the blues began. His parents were sharecroppers; his father left home and his mother died before he was 10. The great bluesman Bukka White was a cousin, but young Riley was more inspired by an aunt's records of Blind Lemon Jefferson and Lonnie Johnson, two of the most famous blues guitarists of the 1920s. In his early teens he went to live in Indianola, Miss., where on Saturday nights he'd stand by the window of a local nightclub and catch glimpses of Count Basie, Louis Jordan, Sonny Boy Williamson (#2) or whomever was working that stop on the "chitlin' circuit" that weekend. He joined a local gospel group, but soon found he could collect a few badly needed coins by singing and playing blues guitar on a local street corner, doing songs he heard on records and on the radio. T-Bone Walker's tasty, jazz-tinged electric guitar playing was a special inspiration, which he tried his darndest to copy. He did the same when he heard the great jazzman Charlie Christian, and when a buddy of his brought him some records by the Belgian gypsy jazz guitarist Django Reinhardt. He never felt he could quite get any of them right, as he modestly says in his autobiography. All the while, of course, he was building his own style, which had lit-

B.B.KING

KING OF THE BLUES

MCA 4-10677, 4 CD's)
A solid compilation covering his whole career, though the pre-1962 years are a bit scantily represented.

THE BEST OF B. B. KING

(MCA 31040)
A single disc of his greatest post-1962 hits.

B. B. KING: LIVE AT THE REGAL

(MCA 31106)
The live album that made the critics rave, and with good reason.

B. B. KING: SINGIN' THE BLUES

(Virgin-Flair 86296)
A good selection of his pre-1962 music.

BOOK: THE B. B. KING COMPANION
ed. by Richard Kostelanetz

(1997, Schirmer Books)
An anthology of articles about B. B., taken from newspapers, learned journals and everything in between, from 1952 to 1996. Includes numerous interviews with the man himself, and a very early magazine piece by the author of the book you're holding. Indexed.

BOOK: BLUES ALL AROUND ME — THE AUTOBIOGRAPHY OF
B. B. KING, by B. B. King with David Ritz.

B. B.'s frank but graceful, eloquent and entertaining life story — with his revealing words on the music he loves, the people who've wounded and supported him, and plenty of war stories from his decades on the road (including a few X-rated ones). Indexed.

tle bits of all of those people plus Blind Lemon and Lonnie Johnson…but it was mostly Riley B. King, and highly original. He even tried using a bottleneck like cousin Bukka used, but it never felt right to him. Instead he learned to bend the notes with his fingers, so that he could make the guitar "talk" with the cadences of speech as well as of music. If any one thing is the essence of his playing, that's it…that, and economy of expression. Unlike many of his imitators he never shows off on guitar, never plays any more notes than necessary to make his point. (That's the way T-Bone played too.)

All the while, of course, he was also learning to sing. Remember, he was in a gospel group, which got to be fairly well known around Indianola. Though he was far from being the first bluesman to grow up with gospel, no one in memory had sung blues with quite as much church feeling as he eventually did.

When he was 23, Indianola started feeling awfully small to him. He headed for Memphis, the nearest big city and a mecca for blues, then as now.* He talked himself into a guest spot on Sonny Boy's live radio show, where he made enough of an impression that he got a paying gig in a local joint that very night, and a rival radio station hired him the very next day. Soon he was also doing a shift as a disc jockey, reveling in the music. The station called him

The Beale Street Blues Boy, which got slimmed down to Blues Boy and then B.B.

Within a year he'd made his first record, a song dedicated to his wife, "Miss Martha King." It was a learning experience. It didn't sell much, and neither did his next seven singles…but with number nine, a version of Lowell Fulson's "3 O'Clock Blues," B. B. suddenly had a national #1 R&B hit on his hands. A good song and a great vocal made the difference. It was late 1951, and B.B. hit the road, where it seems he's been ever since—the man is the ultimate road warrior, playing 200, 250 one-nighters a year, year in and year out.

The hits came one after another for almost a decade. By the early 1960s, though, blues' core audience of African-Americans was aging and shrinking. Younger blacks preferred soul music and funk. Old rural blues like cousin Bukka White's and electric blues like Muddy Waters' were winning a growing cult following among younger whites, but that audience initially rejected B.B.'s music as being too "commercial." Two things turned people's heads in his direction: a stunning live album recorded in Chicago in 1964 (*Live at the Regal*) and the unqualified support of rock heavyweights like the Rolling Stones and promoter Bill Graham. Meanwhile, "The Thrill Is Gone," a sad song that B.B. made a whole lot better, gave him a crossover hit single in 1970 and lots of radio exposure.

By the mid-1980s B.B. had outlived or outlasted most of his contemporaries, and out-performed the rest of them; he'd become unquestionaly the world's most famous living bluesman. And the greatest, many

---

*Around that time (late 1940s), a great many Mississippians headed for an even bigger blues mecca, Chicago. The Windy City didn't have much attraction for young B.B., though. Something about the weather.

would agree. The measure of his greatness is not just his records or even his live shows, but also his influence on others, which is second to none in the entire history of blues…and the way he's made people *respect* blues and the people who sing and play it.

◆

If Mississippi is the home of the blues, North Dakota is about the last state in the U.S.A. you'd expect a bluesman to come from. But that's where **Jonny Lang** (1981-) was born and raised. His *Lie To Me* was the best-selling blues CD in America in 1997, and *Wander This World* matched that feat in 1998

Notice that birthdate—Jonny was only 15 when *Lie To Me* was recorded and released. Younger people have made blues records, but not many. Jonny heard his first blues from his family's record collection, just like B.B.King did. In his early teens, he decided to be a blues singer and guitarist. Jaws drop

when he plays guitar, but his voice is the true knock-out. Most people think it's the voice of someone two or three times his age. On *Wander This World* especially, Jonny Lang's blues has much more in common with the gospel-rooted "soul blues" movement (see p. 194) than with the guitar heroics of such earlier white stars as Eric Clapton and Stevie Ray Vaughan.

Does he make you believe he's "*lived* the blues," whatever that is? That's between you and Jonny. He (and his producer, presumably) choose songs that don't strain that belief (nothing about pickin' cotton or drinkin' whiskey, for instance). He does do one fine old-time blues, "Good Morning Little School Girl," written by Sonny Boy Williamson #1 before 1937. (Lang borrows the arrangement of Howlin' Wolf's 1959 record of "Howlin' For My Darlin'" for this song. Borrowing is an honored tradition in blues. Plagiarism is something attorneys dream up.)

Today, there are blues singers and players like Jonny (if not always quite so young or so talented) in cities all over the world. Not so long ago, most folks thought true blues could only be properly sung and played by people of a certain race, with a

JONNY LANG

LIE TO ME

(A&M 31454 0640)

WANDER THIS WORLD

(A&M 31454 0984)

certain cultural background. Even now it can't be denied that blues recorded long ago by African-Americans from the rural South (or sung today by the few remaining survivors of the pre-WWII blues scene) has a spirit and style that is very hard to replicate, and has a very special place in the hearts of many listeners. However, most would agree that the blues now belongs to everyone. Good, satisfying blues can be sung and played by anyone with talent and dedication, and enjoyed by anyone who cares to listen.

◆

You can hear live blues at least one night a week in practically any town big enough to have nightclubs. In a sizable city you'll probably have three or four acts to choose from any night of the week. For many people, though, the best blues experience is at a blues festival, where you can enjoy half a dozen acts or more, often outdoors. There were more than 150 blues festivals in the U.S.A. in 2000, from the Big Sur Biker Blues Festival in California and the Big Bull Falls Blues Festival in Wausau, Wisconsin to the four-day Chicago Blues Festival in June and the trailblazing Ann Arbor Blues and Jazz Festival in September. Most festivals feature a mix of nationally known and local performers, and the bigger ones will usually have a large range of different blues styles represented, with a mix of younger artists and veterans, often including legendary figures from the 1950s or even earlier.

No CD can match the experience of hearing really good blues live in the flesh…experiencing the creative process as it happens, being a part of the blues community. To this day, many blues artists live for the road. Playing live is what it's all about; CDs are something they put out to help get more live gigs. It's a lot different from the way pop music works these days.

However, for a lot of great and irreplaceable blues artists, from Blind Lemon Jefferson to Johnny Copeland, recordings are all we have now (along with films and videos, in some cases). To hear how the blues got to where it is today, we listen to records. While blues today has a cherished stability to it, there were times in the past when blues changed very rapidly. Records were the main forces for change. Hit records (and even non-hits) affected the evolution of the music in countless ways, for better and for worse. We'll try and trace some of that as we go along. Blues recordings, new and old, are readily available nowadays like they never have been before. We'll use a line or two every now and then to recommend some of the best ones.

What the Heck Is "Blues" Anyway?

The word "blues" predates the music we're talking about by a good bit. It was used as long ago as the 18th century to mean "a feeling of depression or melancholy"…something that sneaks up on most all of us now and then, sometimes without any explainable cause.

When a new style of music came along whose lyrics often spoke of depression or melancholy, that old word was an obvious good fit. When a blues singer begins a song with "I got the blues" (or "I got the Dallas blues," "I got the railroad blues," "I got the broke and hungry blues," etc.) he or she is using the word in the old way.

We'll never know who first attached the name to the musical genre, but it was quite firmly attached in the African-American vernacular well before the establishment culture became aware of it, which it did after several songs written and published by W. C. Handy with "blues" in their titles ("Memphis Blues," "St. Louis Blues") became popular in the second decade of the 20th century.

◆

Aside from being the word that identifies the kind(s) of music covered in this book, the word "blues" has several other strictly musical meanings, which have been known to cause confusion.

The Blues Chorus

The majority of blues songs, though by no means all, have a distinct structure which is often called "the blues chorus." Any song with this structure can be called a blues, regardless of whether it is performed in a style that would be properly called blues.

A blues chorus is designed around a three-line stanza of lyrics. The second line is typically a repeat of the first. The third line almost always provides some sort of conclusion to the thought expressed in the first pair of lines, so that the stanza stands on its own as a statement. (That's one reason why certain blues stanzas pop up in many different songs.)

This three-line stanza also has a distinct musical pattern of twelve measures, or bars, four bars to each line. The first four bars (line one) are sung and played to the tonic chord, the one that has the same name as the key the piece is in. In the key of C, that's a C chord. For the first two bars of line two, the subdominant or IV chord is used—in the key of C, that's F—before returning to the tonic for the next two bars. The last line begins with one bar of the dominant or V chord—G, in the key of C—followed by one more of the subdominant (F) before returning to the tonic for the final two bars of the chorus.

Note that in the last line the dominant (G) does not go directly to the tonic (C). That's one of the most distinctive things about blues, musicologically speaking. Other kinds of music do that all the time—it's probably THE most popular chord change—but it's uncommon in blues.

Over the years, that basic harmonic structure has been subject to infinite variations, especially by jazz musicians, who get impatient when asked to play four bars in the tonic in the first line of each stanza, for instance.

The Blue Note

Musicologists have often commented on the frequent appearance in blues of a note that is not in the standard Western musical scale. This tone—often called "the blue note"—is, in the key of C, halfway between E-flat and E. It gives the music a sound that is neither major nor minor, but something else—the sound of blues.

Rather than hitting that in-between note and holding it, blues singers and guitarists will usually bend or slide their way into and out of the blue note. Pianists cannot actually play the blue note, of course, but blues pianists will often allude to it by playing E-flat and E together or in close proximity.

A second "blue note," this one halfway between B-flat and B in the key of C, is also often heard in blues.

There's More...

After W. C. Handy's songs became pop and jazz favorites in the teens and '20s, numerous songs appeared with "blues" in the title that have little or nothing to do with the music this book is about, like "Limehouse Blues," "Sugar Blues" and "Lovesick Blues" (the vaudeville ditty that later became a hit for country legend Hank Williams Sr., who also recorded numerous authentic blues songs).

From the mid-1920s to the early 1950s, white country singers and bands performed many songs in an often remarkably fine approximation of true blues style (see "Can Blue Men Sing the Whites?" in Chapter 5) but also attached the word "blues" to songs that have little or nothing to do with what we'd normally use the word for.

If you find the English word "blues" on the label of a record released to the Latin American market in the 1950s, it's most likely not a blues at all, but a translation of a sentimental love song from the U.S.A. Hit Parade.

PART ONE

WHO INVENTED THE BLUES?

Chapter 1
Blues Origins

There's no shortage of information about blues today. Books, magazines and websites can tell you practically anything you might want to know. You can find out beyond the shadow of a doubt exactly where Jonny Lang's appearing a week from Friday, who was in B.B. King's band in 1965, or what day Bessie Smith recorded "Back Water Blues."

What you won't find is who invented blues. The fact is, nobody really knows exactly how, when and where the blues began. Eminent researchers have spent a lot of time and energy searching for the origins of blues, and have given us some great insights into the environment that nurtured blues, but there's no smoking gun…far from it.

It must have been exciting when it happened, because the word spread fast and far…too fast for anyone to write down the details, let alone put out records. By the time blues was recognized in any medium that has survived, the horse was far down the road.

The fact that African America was still predominantly an oral culture in those days had something to do with that, but not everything. White people heard blues too, early and often. But to them it was idle entertainment…exciting, yes, but not something to take seriously and write an article about. The literate leaders of the black community had very much the same attitude. Educated Americans still clung to the notion they'd had since before the Revolution—that the only true musical culture was European musical culture, and the only African-American music worth preserving was that which could be made into something "European"…like concert arrangements of spirituals.

So…the early development of blues took place in an information vacuum. However, we can say for (reasonably) sure that…

Blues began taking shape right around the year 1900.

Blues was invented by African-Americans, descendants of the millions of Africans who were forcibly transported to the United States as slaves in the 18th and 19th centuries.

Blues also has important European elements. Blues is sung in English, and played primarily on instruments of European design.

Blues is obviously distinct from anything white Americans were singing or playing at the time of its origin. It seems safe to say that **African influences account for some of this distinction**, even though today's indigenous African music doesn't much resemble blues.

Tracing that influence through history has not been easy. Nobody in the U.S.A. paid much attention to whatever music the slaves sang or played when they arrived in this country, or for many years thereafter. Even from the late 19th century we have only spotty documentation of rural African-American music, often written by people with little understanding of what they chanced to hear.

By the time serious efforts were made to document the African ancestry of blues in the 1950s, it was almost too late. Few African-Americans performed or even remembered their traditional music the way it had sounded before commercial influences (radio and records) changed it profoundly. Nevertheless, in 1959 researcher Alan Lomax was able to find, record and even film a few rural singers and musicians playing music from the pre-blues era with some striking African aspects. His book *The Land Where the Blues Began* (Pantheon Books, 1993) pieces together convincing theories about blues' early development, based on his extensive field recording experience in the U.S.A. and abroad, dating back to the 1930s. An accompanying video contains some of the films he made.

Lomax found roots of blues in many places. One of them is the gigantic levee that protects the Mississippi Delta farmlands (and adjoining areas in other states) from flooding. According to Lomax, the calls of the African-American mule drivers ("muleskinners") who built this levee are "the only clearly African melodies we have found in the United States" and "appear to be the direct ancestors of the blues." (page 212).

He also finds blues roots in the "hollers" of black prisoners in Mississippi and nearby states. They sang in groups to lighten their work load, and also "hollered" individually, each man in his own style—a tradition that lasted into the 1960s. "The traditional blues melodies," Lomax writes, "are in fact holler cadences, set to a steady beat and thus turned into dance music and confined to a three-verse rhymed stanza of twelve to sixteen bars." (page 275).

Perhaps the most remarkable African survivals Lomax found were some dance tunes he recorded (and filmed) at country dances in the hills of north-central Mississippi, just east of the Delta. His book details similarities between this music and music he heard in Africa, and also notes similarities in the way people danced to it.

Sometime around the late 1890s, somewhere around northern Mississippi, people started combining some of those lonesome hollers and mule calls with some of those dance tunes…and what we know as blues came into being. One by one, more people started singing and playing this new style. It spread slowly at first, then about as quickly as any new music could have spread without the help of modern media. By about 1907 blues was the most popular secular music of the African-American rural South, and was rapidly spreading elsewhere, constantly changing as it interacted with other forms of music. One branch of the blues made its way to New York City by way of Memphis. With the music business—sheet music and records—being concentrated in New York, that branch naturally accounted for the blues' first nationwide publicity and the first blues recordings. We'll address that New York blues shortly (see "Money Blues") but first we need to honor the singers who were present at the genesis, or close to it.

✦

What did rural Southern African-Americans sing and play before the coming of blues? Lots of different things.

In slavery days, black slaves provided much music for their owners and for their fellow slaves. With no records, radio or TV available, good musicians were an asset to any home, and the homes of wealthy slave-owners were no exception. Slave musicians were given European-style musical instruments—violins were most popular—and taught to play them in the European manner, primarily for dancing. Naturally enough, they gradually developed distinctive variations on the European pieces they learned, and composed new ones of their own, often playing them on home-made fiddles—and also on what appears to be an early African-American invention, the banjo.

After Emancipation, the music continued. In large and small towns alike across the South, there were concert brass bands of black musicians, similar to those heard throughout white America at the time, and dance bands that combined brass and string instruments. In the 1890s, an especially lively and innovative black dance band scene developed in New Orleans, leading to the music the world would soon revere as "jazz." (As we shall see, jazz and blues have enjoyed a long and fruitful co-existence, each idiom profoundly influencing the other in many ways. But they began separately.)

Rural African-Americans also used stringed instruments to accompany solo and group singing—fiddles, banjos, mandolins and, later, guitars. Most of the songs they sang before the Civil War are lost to history, though a few were picked up by the popular "Ethiopian minstrel" shows (see box on p. 27) and a few more were preserved by folklore collectors.

We do have a much better idea of what the solo vocal repertoire was like just about the time the blues began. That's because several fine singers who learned the music of that era as they were growing up were able to record what they remembered in later years—men like Henry Thomas, Gus Cannon, Furry Lewis, and the mighty Lead Belly. Known as "songsters" by latterday historians, these artists sang primarily story songs and dance tunes, along with varying quantities of Tin Pan Alley pop songs, children's songs and religious material. They also recorded blues, which leads to an interesting guessing game as we try to figure out which of their songs represent the very earliest stages of blues, and which ones they learned or composed later on, after blues became widely popular.

The oldest songster to make records was apparently Johnny Watson, known as Daddy Stovepipe, born in Alabama between 1867 and 1870. His records offer no great revelations, but those of **Henry Thomas ("Ragtime Texas")** (1874-ca. 1930) are a terrific time machine, a fascinating, entertaining window to the past.

Thomas sang lively dance tunes accompanied by guitar and a set of reed pipes, called "quills" or "panpipes," whose joyful sound was imitated by Canned Heat on the 1968 hit "Goin' Up The Country" (it's Thomas' "Bull Doze Blues" with new lyrics). Of his 23 surviving recordings, made between 1927 and 1929, four would fit most of the qualifications for being blues (see pp. 14-15). Others hail from the rich vein of 19th century folksong. "John Henry" is here, the indestructible song about the nearly indestructible Superman of railroad workers that still reigns as the best-known African-American folksong. So are a couple of delightful children's songs, "The Little Red Caboose" (its first-ever recording) and "Fishing Blues," the modern day Taj Mahal favorite. (This is not a blues at all—in the 1920s and 1930s, record companies followed their commercial instincts and indiscriminately tagged all sorts of songs as blues.)

In between the definite blues and the definite non-blues are songs like "Don't Ease Me In" and "Shanty Blues," which are probably typical of what else was being sung by the same people who sang the first blues. You could call them brothers and sisters of blues, from the same gene pool…songs that coex-

HENRY THOMAS

TEXAS WORRIED BLUES
COMPLETE RECORDED WORKS, 1927–1929

(Yazoo 1080/1)
All there is, no more, no less…antique but irresistible.

isted with blues until the latter clearly established itself as the pick of the litter, which didn't happen until Thomas' musical career was well under way.

The words "rag" and "ragtime," by the way, could refer to any fast dance pieces; Thomas' music has little kinship to that of piano ragtime genius Scott Joplin ("Maple Leaf Rag," "The Entertainer") and his ilk.

GUS CANNON

COMPLETE RECORDED WORKS IN CHRONOLOGICAL ORDER, Vol. 1

(Document 5032)
Contains the 1927 Paramount session plus some magnificient jug band recordings.

Next in order of birthdate comes **Gus Cannon** (1883-1979). Cannon is rumored to have made records in 1901, more than two decades before any other rural African-American secular artist visited a recording studio. What we wouldn't give for copies of those unreleased (and presumably lost) sides! He's best remembered as the leader of Cannon's Jug Stom-

pers (see box on p.58) but one record he made in 1927, singing and playing banjo with Blind Blake on guitar, is vintage songster stuff. "Poor Boy Long Ways From Home" is as good a candidate as any for the oldest true blues song; Cannon's version might be the only existing example of bottleneck banjo! (see "bottleneck" on p. 77) The other side is a hilarious, enlightening story-song about Booker T. Washington's visit to the White House.

Sam Collins (1887-1949) recorded mainly blues, which he sang and played in a lyrical manner quite different from the more in-your-face approach of younger Mississippians like Son House, and a sweet bottleneck guitar style (sometimes betrayed by poor guitar tuning). "Do That Thing" is a dance piece with a definite dawn-of-the-blues aura. Among Collins' notable non-blues material is the first (1927) recording of the familiar folksong "Midnight Special."

SAM COLLINS

JAILHOUSE BLUES

(Yazoo 1079)

LEAD BELLY

IN THE SHADOWS OF THE GALLOWS POLE

(Tradition 1018)

Lead Belly was at the top of his game on these late 1930s—early 1940s recordings, which splendidly demonstrate the variety of his repertoire—prison worksongs, children's songs, story songs, and some mean blues. This particular CD has better sound quality than other available reissues of this material, originally made under low-budget conditions.

LEADBELLY'S LAST SESSIONS

(Smithsonian-Folkways 40068/71)

Before Lead Belly's final illness sapped his strength in the late 1940s, there was a concerted effort to record as many of his songs as possible with the brand-new technology of magnetic tape. He might have lost a step compared to a decade earlier, but to hear his music with reasonably high fidelity is an awesome experience.

"Midnight Special" later became one of many signature songs for the king of the songsters, the formidable Huddie Ledbetter, better known as **Lead Belly** (1888-1949).

Lead Belly missed out on the first wave of rural blues recording in the 1920s; he spent much of his early adulthood in prison for homicide. He eventually got released from prison after writing and singing a song for the state governor. In 1930 he was back in the slammer, this time for assault with intent to kill. He was at the Angola State Prison Farm in Louisiana in 1934 when folklorist John A. Lomax and his son Alan visited the prison, looking for traditional music which they recorded for the Library of Congress on primitive portable equipment.

Lead Belly was the find of a lifetime for any folksong collector. He knew hundreds if not thousands of songs—"John Henry," "Midnight Special," folksongs that could be traced back to the British Isles, Tin Pan Alley tunes, dance tunes of every description, prison work songs, mule-skinner hollers, turn-of-the-century "rag" songs, and all manner of blues ranging from the very earliest forms to songs he'd learned from records in the 1920s, and new topical blues he composed whenever he felt the urge. He sang all of these in a roof-rattling high baritone, and accompanied them with a 12-string guitar that roared like a locomotive.

The Lomaxes managed to spring Lead Belly from prison, and hired him as their expedition's chauffeur. At the end of the trip they brought him to New York City, and introduced him to everyone they knew. He soon became, naturally enough, a minor celebrity, and wound up spending most of the rest of his life there. It was not always a happy time; he never became quite the star he deserved to be, and there was rarely enough money. Folk music aficionados idolized him, but the folk music revival was still in its infancy and there weren't very many of them. (Ironically, one of Lead Belly's songs, "Goodnight Irene," would raise the revival to a new level when The Weavers, featuring Pete Seeger, covered it shortly after his death.) Meanwhile, the black mainstream audience of the late 1930s found his music outdated

Two major labels recorded him for this audience, but the records sold poorly.

Nevertheless, Lead Belly managed to get most of his vast repertoire down on wax and tape. Most of what he left us is now available on CD.

There's been no end to the controversy surrounding Lead Belly's life, his moody personality and his uneasy relationship with his new white friends. A fine recent biography, *The Life and Legend of Lead-belly* by Charles Wolfe and Kip Lornell, gives us the details. Likewise, his music remains a bit controversial among blues fans, some of whom write him off a bit too readily as a "folk singer" due to his connections with the revival. He was indeed a "folk singer," in the very best sense of the word, and a damn fine bluesman too when he wanted to be.

Peg Leg Howell (1888-1966) from rural Georgia was one of the first "country blues" artists to record, in 1926. In addition to numerous straight-ahead blues, his recordings include the delightful "Skin

JIM JACKSON

COMPLETE RECORDED WORKS IN CHRONOLOGICAL ORDER, Volume 1

(Document 5114)

FRANK STOKES

CREATOR OF THE MEMPHIS BLUES

(Yazoo 1056)

Game Blues" (not a blues but a turn-of-the-century song about gambling, with sinuous slide guitar) and some lively dance tunes with Eddie Anthony on fiddle. The latter sides are an echo, perhaps, of the distant days when the fiddle was the most popular instrument among African-Americans.

Jim Jackson (1890-1937) travelled the South with minstrel and medicine shows but eventually settled in Memphis. He had a wide repertoire of minstrel ditties ("I Heard the Voice of a Porkchop") and folk songs, but made his mark with "Jim Jackson's Kansas City Blues," probably the top-selling guitar blues disc of 1927. The song's memorable, oft-repeated hook line ("I'm gonna move, babe—honey, where they don't 'low you,") and its stripped-down guitar accompaniment with its relentless medium-slow beat were very much a preview of the way blues would evolve in the next few years after it was made. Though he also recorded some truly delightful songster pieces and 1910-era blues ("I'm Wild About My Lovin'," "This Morning She Was Gone"), Jackson goes down in history as guitar blues' first one-hit wonder.

Frank Stokes (1888-1955) was another favorite Memphis songster in the 1920s, singing hoary minstrel ditties and up-to-date blues in his sonorous baritone, and playing guitar with an irresistible dance beat.

Furry Lewis (ca. 1893-1981) was born in Greenwood, Miss. Though he spent most of his life in Memphis, his old-time country songster style never changed—to the delight of countless new fans who saw and heard him in concert, on TV or in the movies in his later years. As a young man, Furry paid his dues and learned his craft as an entertainer for "medicine shows" that toured the rural South (see box). His late 1920s recordings included such songster staples as "John Henry," "Stackerlee" and "Kassie [i.e. Casey] Jones," in addition to many splendid blues. His music was already a bit old-fashioned by then, though, and he gradually faded from the music scene, working for forty years as a street cleaner for the city of Memphis.

FURRY LEWIS

IN HIS PRIME

(Yazoo 1050)

Furry was the first of more than a dozen 1920s blues recording artists who were "rediscovered" after years of obscurity and introduced to 1960s folk revival audiences. Another great one was **Mississippi John Hurt** (1893-1966), whose soft, deep voice enchanted folk revival audiences while his fluent, complex fingerpicking drove novice guitarists to despair. Mississippi John never meant to be a professional entertainer; he was content to sing and play songs like "Casey Jones" and "Nobody's Dirty Business" at

MISSISSIPPI JOHN HURT

1928 Sessions

(Yazoo 1065)
All the surviving sides from his OKeh sessions.

THE BEST OF MISSSISSIPPI JOHN HURT

(Vanguard VCD 19/20) A fine selection of the artist's later work.

weekend picnics while earning a living as a farmhand in and around Avalon, Miss., in the hill country east of the Delta. However, in 1928 some country musicians who lived nearby recommended John to OKeh Records. The records didn't sell much, but by the early 1960s tape copies were being passed around the folk community like words from heaven. In 1963 the man himself was located, still herding cows outside Avalon and singing and playing just like he always had. He spent most of his last three years on the folk festival and coffeehouse circuit, and recorded three fine LPs.

John Hurt was among the youngest of the men we count among the great "songsters," artists who performed a wide variety of songs old and new in addition to blues.

We know that many younger singers also performed folksongs and pop tunes—those who saw **Robert Johnson** (1911-1938) live, for instance, clearly remember him singing "My Blue Heaven." However, the same early recording directors who were happy to record a Henry Thomas or a John Hurt singing folksongs and other pre-blues items generally asked for and got only blues (and the occasional religious piece) from rural singers born after 1895. Blues had taken over, and the South (and the world) would never be quite the same again.

VARIOUS ARTISTS

BEFORE THE BLUES, Vols. 1/3

(Yazoo 2015/7)

A fascinating assemblage of records from the 1920s and 1930s that appear in one way or another to represent Southern rural music from 1900 or earlier. Henry Thomas, Peg Leg Howell, Sam Collins, Mississippi John Hurt, and numerous lesser-known songsters and blues singers are represented, along with black rural dance musicians. There's a lot of emphasis on traditions that were shared by blacks and whites, with examples by artists of both races. The CDs are programmed more according to listening pleasure than educational logic; each of the three separately available CDs, for instance, has one or two tracks featuring black fiddlers.

Ethiopian Minstrels

We must mention, at least in passing, the "Ethiopian minstrel" shows that were America's most popular form of musical theatre for much of the 19th century. ("Ethiopian" in this context simply meant "black"—there was no direct connection with the East African nation.) Minstrel shows consisted of songs, dances and comedy dialogue performed primarily by white performers dressed as caricatures of blacks, complete with "blackface" makeup. Relying as they did on outrageous stereotypes, minstrel shows are often cited today as a uniquely odious skeleton in America's cultural closet…but their initial inspiration was real-life African-American music, and it was the minstrels that gave white America its very first mass exposure to black music, if only in secondhand fashion—thus laying the groundwork for the later popularity of blues and jazz. And as time went on, more actual black performers could be seen and heard in minstrel shows. A few minstrel songs, written by whites, are still sung today—"Turkey In the Straw," "Dixie" and especially the songs of Stephen Foster, like "Oh Susannah," "Camptown Races" and "My Old Kentucky Home."

Medicine Shows

"Medicine shows" were frequent visitors to small towns throughout the U.S.A., including the South, in the early 20th century. They were organized by "doctors" to promote and sell tonics and other concoctions which today's FDA would definitely not approve of. They'd arrive on a wagon or a flatbed truck which they'd set up in the center of town. The medicine show would begin with free entertainment, usually music of some kind. Once the music had drawn a crowd, the "doctor" would make his pitch for snake oil, or whatever he happened to be selling, take the people's hard-earned money, and roll on to the next town. Quite a few bluesmen got their start in medicine shows, along with country singers and all sorts of other entertainers both black and white.

Where's the Guitar?

It's hard to even think of Southern rural African-American music without guitars. However, guitars were not common among black musicians in the area much before 1900.

In 19th-century America the guitar was associated with soft, gentle music in the parlor. The guitars available in the 19th century were small, and strung with catgut rather than steel. They had little volume, and were not much use for dance music—fiddles and banjos were the choice for that. They also weren't well-suited for the black vocal music of the day…a catgut-strung guitar just didn't have enough testosterone for a proper "John Henry."

Late in the 19th century, bigger, louder, more robust steel-stringed guitars made their way into the Southeast from Mexico via Texas, where they were introduced to the locals by Mexican *vaqueros* (cowboys). These instruments were soon imitated and improved by American manufacturers, and advertised in the ubiquitous Sears-Roebuck catalog.

The advent of the steel-string guitar was probably a major reason why blues was born when and where it was. Here, finally, was a portable instrument that could make a one-man vocal-instrumental performance not only more danceable than a banjo could, but more expressive—a whole lot more expressive. So it encouraged the singing of songs that were more expressive, more emotional. Right there you have one of the main things that distinguishes blues from what came before.

Guitar notes sustain (ring out) much longer than banjo notes…which means a guitar player has much more chance to "bend" them, to vary the pitch as the note sounds, making it sing, making it talk, making it cry, almost like a human voice.

"So black country guitar pickers taught their instruments to sing the blues," wrote Alan Lomax, "and, at the same time, to serve as one-piece dance orchestras, evoking the multiple patterns of the old-time string band by beating, picking, plucking, hammering, pushing and sliding. This new six-string virtuosity so fascinated the black working class that a lone bluesman with a guitar was enough for a dance or a party. His music kept everybody happily on the dance floor and his lyrics, sung and picked, told everybody's story."

Low-Class Music

"All Negroes like blues!" So said Lead Belly, introducing "Good Morning Blues" to his mostly white listeners on one of his later recordings. He overstated the case a bit. Blues did indeed become popular with African-Americans, but the verdict was far from unanimous.

Blues was originated and initially consumed by poor rural black folk, just about the lowest of the low in America's de facto caste system. Blues singers were often little more than penniless beggars, drifting from town to town. Even those who made some money were regarded as uncouth rascals—a stereotype some of them admittedly lived up to with their hard drinking, brawling and womanizing. Middle-

and upper-class blacks found bluesmen even more distasteful than whites did, disdaining their music as illiterate trash. Moreover, many blacks of all economic strata regarded blues as sinful and immoral.

Over the years blues very gradually became more respectable…though it always lagged well behind its city cousin, jazz. Just compare the kinds of venues where blues was heard in the 1930s, 1940s and 1950s to the comparatively elegant clubs that welcomed jazz. Thankfully, that's changed. As blues gets the respect it's long deserved from fans of all races and classes, it can now point with self-confidence and a bit of pride to its down-home working-class origins.

Parallels to the Blues

African slaves were also imported to many other parts of the New World besides the United States, especially Brazil and the Caribbean. In every one of these areas, these slaves and their descendants adopted and adapted the local music, changing it profoundly and

creating new hybrids. The development of samba in Brazil, calypso in Trinidad and mento, ska and reggae in Jamaica closely parallels the history of blues and jazz in the United States.

PART TWO

MONEY BLUES

Chapter 2

Blues Becomes a Business

W. C. Handy, Vaudeville, and the First Blues Records

W. C. Handy

The very, very first blues might have been sung for the pure pleasure and catharsis of it…but it wasn't long before people discovered they could get paid for singing blues. It was inevitable that sooner or later blues would become a business, for better or worse. We don't know who was the first to make a comfortable living from singing blues. Most likely it was a singer with one of the black vaudeville companies somewhere around 1910. It just might have been Ma Rainey, who was still going strong when the record companies discovered blues a decade later.

We do know that the first person to gain nationwide fame and significant fortune from blues was W. C. Handy—William Christopher Handy, born in Florence, Alabama, in 1873. He called himself "Father of the Blues," and he was born early enough so that he could conceivably have invented blues. Well, he didn't, but there are other reasons blues' highest honor today is called a W. C. Handy Award.

A middle-class African-American trained in classical music, Handy began his career in minstrel shows. After becoming musical direc-

tor of Mahara's Minstrels, he left to start his own brass band, playing pop hits and light classical pieces for dances and concerts. Now and then, in his travels, he heard rural music, including blues. As he told it in his autobiography, he was especially impressed by a shabby, ragged singer-guitarist he encountered in a Mississippi train station in 1903. A few years later, he got around to composing some blues songs. "Memphis Blues," conceived in 1909 as a campaign song for the mayor of Memphis and finally published in 1912, was one of the first blues to be written down and published, and the very first commercial blues song hit.*

Unlike far too many later bluesmen, Handy knew how important it was to own your own songs. With a partner, he started his own publishing company, which grew very prosperous as Handy wrote "Yellow Dog Blues," "Beale Street Blues," and the biggest of them all, "St. Louis Blues." In all of these Handy cleverly dressed up the authentic blues content with "legit" musical elements; there's even a bit of tango in "St. Louis Blues." These songs were all immediate hits with the black vaudeville companies that had forced the old minstrel troupes into retirement, and were featured by white vaudeville singers and dance bands as well. As a successful song composer *and* publisher, W.C. Handy was a big man when he moved to New York in 1918.

---

*The verse of the 1911 Tin Pan Alley hit "Oh You Beautiful Doll" is in the blues' familiar 12-bar form, but this song is not a blues.

Handy didn't write as many hits there as he had in Memphis, but his success was contagious. One who caught the fever was a fellow native Alabaman, **Perry Bradford**. One day Perry had the bright idea that blues songs might be even more successful, and record companies too, if people could buy records of real African-Americans singing this vital African-American music.

It seems incredible today that no blues performed by an African-American was available on records before 1920, when the music had existed for at least two decades. You could buy versions of "Memphis Blues" and "St. Louis Blues" by white singers and bands. You could buy records of Swedish music, Chinese music, Turkish music. You could buy records of Bert Williams, the great black vaudevillian…but not a note of real American blues—or any real country music, for that matter. (About the closest thing to real blues was a 1916 release by white singer George O'Connor, a comically awful rendition of some authentic traditional blues lyrics—titled, unfortunately, "Nigger Blues").

Mamie Smith

The most plausible explanation for this neglect of blues is that the record companies, based in New York, just weren't aware of or interested in what was happening in the hinterlands. They'd done just fine by recording what was available in New York, and just didn't pay much attention to true blues until it landed on their doorstep in the person of Perry Bradford.

Anyhow, Bradford finally talked OKeh Records into recording a black vaudeville singer named Mamie Smith singing some of his songs. What happened when the records were released set the whole industry on its ear. It seemed like all of Harlem lined up outside record stores to get the second single, "Crazy Blues." OKeh and its competitors madly scrambled to find more songs like it, and more African-American singers.

Now "Crazy Blues" was not exactly the blues of the rural South…the blues of Charlie Patton or Blind Lemon Jefferson. The record industry was still a few years away from venturing that far from New York. But that early 1920s vaudeville blues was a smash across African America, and attracted more than a few white fans as well. Within a few years more people had heard it than had ever been exposed to the rural Southern variety.

◆

Like so many other things in 20th century music, that vaudeville blues was a complex hybrid. It mixed W.C. Handy–style blues, already a hybrid itself, with standard Tin Pan Alley pop music, and—crucially— jazz.

In a case of fortuitous timing, New Orleans jazz became a New York sensation the year before W.C. Handy arrived there. While jazz and blues probably didn't have a whole lot to do with each other before 1917—despite a lot of guessing to the contrary in early writings about both blues and jazz—they blended beautifully in Harlem, and on hundreds of fine records made there and elsewhere before the style died out rather abruptly in the late 1920s.

This was the blues of Bessie Smith, Ma Rainey, Clara Smith, Alberta Hunter, Victoria Spivey, Ida Cox, Lucille Hegamin, Rosa Henderson and Sippie Wallace, to name a few. This kind of blues never had a special name back then—it was just "the blues," the only kind you could get on records for a while. Nowadays it's often called "classic blues." Truthfully it's no more "classic" than any other kind of blues; we prefer "vaudeville blues" since black vaudeville is where the style originated and where it was performed.

Notice that all those people we just named were female, dramatically reversing the gender bias of most other kinds of blues. Most of the vaudeville blues songs were written by men, and most of the instrumental accompanists were men, but every vaudeville blues singer of any importance was female. If any male singer seriously tried to move into that territory back then, he wasn't recorded or written about.

Vaudeville blues was performed in New York's speakeasies, and in theatres in black neighborhoods across the country. Most venues were segregated, open to blacks only, but some offered special performances for whites. The stars toured frequently, and by all accounts the performances were something to see. The staging was elaborate, and the women wore fabulous costumes. The vaudeville blues women were among the most celebrated and revered African-Americans of their time.

Bessie Smith (1894-1937) was the most successful of the vaudeville blues singers, and by practically

Vaudeville is the type of stage show that succeeded the minstrel show as the most popular light theatrical entertainment in the U.S.A. near the end of the 19th century. A typical vaudeville show consisted of a dozen or so acts, each performing for five or ten minutes (a little more for the top stars). Patrons usually saw a mix of singers, dancers, instrumentalists, comedians, jugglers, animal acts or anything that was popular at the moment. Vaudeville was intended as family entertainment, and anything that was the slightest bit off-color was prohibited. (Such entertainment could often be found down the street at the local burlesque theatre.)

Al Jolson, who often appeared in blackface, was the supreme star of the vaudeville era. Real African-Americans performed in separate all-black vaudeville companies, offering a mix of entertainment generally similar to the white shows. During the decade between 1910 and 1920, female singers featuring blues songs became popular in black vaudeville, and these women were the first black blues singers of any kind to make records.

The First Black-Owned Record Label

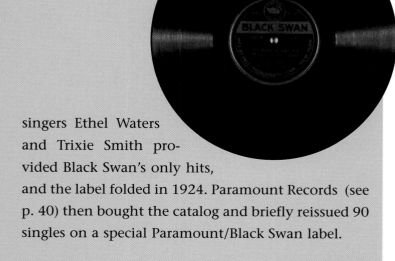

...was Black Swan Records, started in 1921 by W.C. Handy's former business partner, Harry Pace. Black Swan recorded a wide variety of music by African-American artists, including not only jazz and blues but also straight pop and semi-classical music, some Caribbean and South American selections, and even a couple of operatic arias. However, vaudeville blues singers Ethel Waters and Trixie Smith provided Black Swan's only hits, and the label folded in 1924. Paramount Records (see p. 40) then bought the catalog and briefly reissued 90 singles on a special Paramount/Black Swan label.

unanimous consent the best. A big, self-confident woman, she was heavy drinker, a lusty bisexual, the source of a thousand legends. Even her death in a car crash became a legend—it was said that she bled to death because a nearby whites-only hospital wouldn't admit her. Though that wasn't exactly the way it happened, the story became a powerful rallying cry for integration. (Ironically the accident happened near Clarksdale, Miss.—later to become a virtual capital of the blues world.)

However rowdy a character she may have been offstage, when Bessie was performing or recording she was so totally in command of things that "queen of the blues" wasn't quite good enough—Bessie Smith was Empress of the Blues. Setting a slow tempo—most vaudeville blues were slow—she charged every line, every word with drama. At the same time she phrased her blues much like jazz soloists such as Louis Armstrong formed their melodies. It's probably no coincidence at all that Armstrong first established his power as a soloist—which revolutionized jazz—at the same time that Bessie came to power, in the early 1920s. Their collaborations on records are still as stunning as ever, and they clearly fed off each other's creativity.

BESSIE SMITH

Exclusive Columbia Phonograph Artist

Bessie Smith was born in Chattanooga, Tenn. By the time she reached her teens, an older brother was working in a traveling vaudeville show, which featured the great singer Ma Rainey, reputed to have been the first woman to sing blues in

executives (including Thomas Edison) found her style too "rough" (or her skin too dark). Be that as it may, she signed with Columbia in 1923. From the moment her first 78 hit the stores that spring, she blew away the competition artistically and commercially. As with other vaudeville blues women, her years of performing in theatres without a microphone helped give her the decibels she needed to cut through the thick haze of the pre-electronic recording process. Bessie's sense of drama and phrasing made her voice jump right out of the crudest wind-up Victrola.

She wound up recording over 150 songs for Columbia. For the next four years or so, Columbia could hardly press enough to meet the demand. But then the vaudeville blues boom ran out of gas, rather suddenly, and even Bessie Smith was not invincible in the marketplace. The coming of the Great Depression almost annihilated the record business, and in 1931 Columbia decided it couldn't afford Bessie Smith (and her hazardous lifestyle) anymore. (Record producer John Hammond managed to arrange a final session in 1933.) Despite all this, she continued to perform live (quite splendidly, we're told) until her tragic death.

Decades later, Columbia paid her the ultimate compliment of reissuing her entire recorded output, first on LP and then on CD.

vaudeville (some say she was the first woman to sing blues anywhere). After singing on the streets for awhile, Bessie joined the troupe at age 18, initially as a dancer.

We don't know how much of Bessie's style was formed before she joined the troupe in 1912, or what she might have learned from Ma Rainey. It seems likely that Bessie was already singing at least some blues in her street-singing days. We do know that she readily took to life in the theatres, and her singing soon made her a featured attraction. By the time Bessie moved to Philadelphia in 1921, she was singing blues with authority, and her live performances had made her a star throughout the South.

Incredibly enough, Bessie Smith failed her first auditions with record companies. It seems that some

Once Bessie hit the jackpot, **Ma Rainey** (1886-1939) clearly deserved her own chance in the studios, which she got in December 1923 with Paramount

BESSIE SMITH

THE COMPLETE RECORDINGS, Volumes 1–5

(Columbia/Legacy)

Ten CDs in all, and not a bit of filler. Which one to start with? Perhaps Volume II, for the Armstrong collaborations. Bessie's own own composition "Back Water Blues," inspired by news of the great Mississippi floods of 1927, is alone worth the price of Volume III.

Records (see page 40). She was 37 years old then, a veteran of two decades in Southern black vaudeville. It was said that while Bessie may have been a greater singer, Ma Rainey was the greater *performer*. Her legend has grown in recent years due to August Wilson's play *Ma Rainey's Black Bottom* (named after one of her records). (The play is not always historically accurate, but the spirit is there and it will move you.)

As one might expect, Rainey is the "rootsiest" of the 1920s vaudeville blues women, the least influenced by Tin Pan Alley, the closest to rural blues. She made a few sides with guitar accompaniment; if these were all she'd left us, we'd never guess she was in vaudeville. "Shave 'Em Dry Blues," recorded in 1924

with the otherwise obscure Milas Pruitt on 12-string guitar, has a definite "dawn-of-the-blues" feel to it. Pruitt's charging countermelodies on the bass strings sound uncannily like Lead Belly.

On the other hand many of Rainey's records are enlivened by Armstrong, Coleman Hawkins and other top-flight jazz musicians, giving them a contemporary flair for 1920s listeners.

Those records are not always easy to listen to; Paramount's recording technique was much inferior to Columbia's, and some of the reissues of Ma's work are almost painful to hear. But give it a try if you can; you'll hear singing that's rich in feeling along with some nice musicianship, and you'll be hearing some-

Paramount Records

Paramount Records, one of the most important early blues labels, began in 1916 as a subsidiary of the Wisconsin Chair Co. located near Milwaukee. The furniture company had begun making phonographs and decided to branch out into records. Paramount began with ordinary pop music, but in 1921 the company acquired a few recordings of black singers from other labels. The results encouraged Paramount to start making its own "race records" in 1922. Though pop recording continued, records by black artists remained Paramount's specialty from that point on.

Early Paramounts featured vaudeville blues singers and jazz instrumentals. Alberta Hunter was the label's first blues star, joined by Ida Cox and then Ma Rainey. Spirituals by the Norfolk Jubilee Quartet also sold well.

In 1926 Paramount began recording Texas singer-guitarist Blind Lemon Jefferson, the most famous rural bluesman of the 1920s. Paramount subsequently signed many other singer-guitarists, whose visits to Paramount's Wisconsin studios

yielded some of history's finest blues: Blind Blake, Charlie Patton, Son House and Skip James to name just a few. Tampa Red and Big Bill Broonzy both made their recording debuts at Paramount before hitting it big on other labels.

Unfortunately Paramount's expertise in the technical side of recording didn't live up to its excellent taste in blues. Paramounts from 1927-28 have just about the worst sound in the entire record industry at the time, tinny and shrill. The later ones are a little better—but by that time the company was running out of money and the records weren't well distributed. Clean copies of the final issues, which include some of Paramount's greatest blues, are all but impossible to find...and when the company finally closed in 1932, KO'd by the Great Depression, most of the original masters were thrown away.

Race Records: What's in a Name

Ever since record companies started making records expressly for the African-American market in the early 1920s, the industry has felt a need for a name to distinguish these records from other releases.

It wasn't just the records for black Americans that were segregated. Labels also had separate series of records in many foreign languages, and also for records of what we now call country music.

What did they call the records for African-Americans? In the early years, all the labels called them "race records." Not "Negro records" or "black records" or "colored records"; it was always "race records."

It was a euphemism, an unnecessary and odious euphemism by today's standards. But it was a term that black as well as white leaders found acceptable at the time. The black press of that era often referred to African-Americans collectively as "the Race"—"Jesse Owens is the greatest athlete of the Race."

Record companies printed booklets listing their "race records," often with dime-sized photos of the artists; these are priceless collectibles today. Gospel-spiritual records are included along with blues, and often some jazz as well. Even records by white artists occasionally found their way into the race series, including a Columbia release the Allen Brothers (country singers who sued the label over this gaffe) and Paramount sides by jazzmen Charles Pierce and Boyd Senter.

It was only after WWII that the term "race records" began to seem distasteful to many in the industry and elsewhere. But what else to call them? *Billboard* magazine decided the case with its issue of June 25, 1949, in which the chart that had been called "Best Selling Race Records" became "Best Selling Rhythm & Blues Records." (In the same issue, the erstwhile "folk" chart became "Country & Western".)

"Rhythm & blues," soon abbreviated to "R & B," was an apt description of what that part of the record industry was selling at that time: jump tunes by Louis Jordan, Julia Lee and Joe Liggins, and blues. "R & B" was part of every hip young music fan's vernacular in the 1950s. In 1969, with soul singers dominating the R&B market, *Billboard* changed the chart name to "Best Selling Soul Singles." In 1982 it became the "Black Music" chart—but in recent years it's been "R&B" once again; never mind that the music on that chart little resembles what was called R&B a half-century ago. (*Billboard* now keeps a separate "Blues" chart, listing best-selling blues CDs regardless of the performer's race.)

one who was there when blues began, or awfully close to it.

Sippie Wallace (1898-1986) grew up in Texas and New Orleans, in a family of jazz musicians. Her brother Hersal Thomas was a celebrated piano prodigy who died at 16 of food poisoning. Her 1920s records are studded with great jazz soloists—Armstrong, Sidney Bechet, King Oliver. After many years as a church soloist, Wallace returned to blues in the 1960s. The young Bonnie Raitt was much inspired by her comeback LPs and returned the favor by appearing on Wallace's W.C. Handy Award–winning album *Sippie* in 1982.

Ethel Waters (1896-1977) scored the first and biggest hit for the ill-fated black-owned Black Swan record label (see box) with "Down Home Blues," recorded in the spring of 1921. That title notwithstanding, she quickly became more identified with the pop side of black vaudeville singing, recording only an occasional blues. She did become an excellent pop singer, then a distinguished actress. For the last

SIPPIE WALLACE

SIPPIE

(Atlantic SD 81592)

MA RAINEY

MA RAINEY'S BLACK BOTTOM

(Yazoo 1071)

A fine cross-section of the singer's work. Yazoo, as usual, squeezes the most lifelike sound possible from these antique sides.

two decades of her life she toured and performed with evangelist Billy Graham.

Victoria Spivey (1906-1976) is often identified as a vaudeville or "classic" singer. However, she was a decade or more younger than the others mentioned here, and it made a difference. Unlike many of the vaudevillians, she wrote her own material, which is full of vivid lines about real-life situations from cocaine sniffing to dried-up alligator ponds. She cut her first record at age

Ethel Waters

City. After some years of semi-retirement, she started her own record company in 1962, recording contemporary blues along with her own singing, and that of other veterans such as Sippie Wallace and Lucille Hegamin. One early Spivey Records session featured the young Bob Dylan on harmonica.

19 in St. Louis in 1926, playing her own piano accompaniment. "Black Snake Blues" was one of the year's biggest hits, and Spivey continued putting out simple, down-to-earth blues for awhile before turning to jazz and the musical stage at the end of the decade when she settled in New York

VICTORIA SPIVEY

VICTORIA SPIVEY: 1926–1931

(Document 590)

BLUES MASTERS, Vol. 11: CLASSIC BLUES WOMEN

(Rhino 71134)

Bessie, Ma, Trixie, Sippie, Victoria Spivey and more, in a solid one-disc sampler of the vaudeville genre.

Chapter **3**
From the Hinterlands

By 1924 the so-called "race records" industry was well established, with most of the larger record companies regularly releasing product expressly intended for the African-American market. With vaudeville blues, hot dance music, and religious records all moving in profitable quantities, the labels began looking for whatever else they could sell.

The record moguls were vaguely aware of rural blues, but they doubted that many of its listeners could afford to spend 75¢ (close to $10 in today's money) for a record. They had felt the same about rural white music…but when a homespun disc by Georgia's Fiddlin' John Carson sold well into six figures in 1923, they changed their mind in a hurry about that.

Not surprisingly, the first blues singer-guitarists to become record stars were not strictly rural. The first hit blues record by a male singer was 1924's "Salty Dog," a Paramount

Lonnie Johnson with Blind John Davis

release by **Papa Charlie Jackson** (c. 1890-c. 1938). Papa Charlie came from New Orleans and was singing on the streets of Chicago when a Paramount man came across him. He usually played a banjo-guitar, a six-string instrument played like a guitar but with a head from a banjo. It was louder than a standard guitar but not as expressive. He did best with uptempo dance blues—"Shake That Thing" (1925) was another smash. He had regular Paramount releases until 1930, and a pair for another label in 1934; no one knows for sure what became of him after that. He was kind of a Jazz Age songster rather than a great bluesman, but his success opened the door for other blues-singing men with string instruments.

Before moving on to the rural bluesmen who began recording in the mid-1920s, let us salute a truly great and quite unclassifiable singer-guitarist from the city of New Orleans, who was equally at home with jazz and blues. **Lonnie Johnson** (1894-1970) was born and raised in New Orleans during that city's heyday as the center of jazz. His father had a string band, in which Lonnie played first violin and then guitar. He went to London with a musical revue, and returned to find that virtually his entire family had died in the great 1919 flu epidemic. He moved to St. Louis where he played in jazz bands and began singing blues. In 1925 he won a blues contest, the prize being an OKeh recording contract.

During the next seven years Johnson recorded over 100 vocal blues, with solo guitar or small group backing. OKeh also happened to be recording a couple of pretty fair jazzmen, Louis Armstrong and Duke Ellington; Johnson recorded with both of them. Along the way he found time to accompany Victoria Spivey on many sides, and also a rural bluesman named Texas Alexander. He also recorded several stunning guitar solos, more jazz than blues, as were his duets with the era's top white jazz guitarist, Eddie Lang.

Details about Johnson's live performance career back then are sketchy, but it's said that he toured with Bessie Smith and also played with various jazz

LONNIE JOHNSON

STEPPIN' ON THE BLUES

(Columbia 46221)

bands as well as singing blues. The recording scene dried up during the Depression, but in 1937 he began recording blues again with moderate success, which continued after World War II.

In 1948, quite out of the blue, Lonnie Johnson had the #1 R&B record in the country, and a major crossover pop hit as well...not singing blues, mind you, but crooning a forgotten 1939 pop tune called "Tomorrow Night." That jump-started the career for a while, but Lonnie was working as a hotel janitor in 1960 when record producer/historian Chris Albertson signed him to make an LP. That led to fairly steady work on the blues revival circuit for the rest of his life, though audiences and critics didn't always know what to make of him. They expected an old black man with a guitar to sing rough and ready blues from the cotton-fields. Lonnie Johnson never sang or played that way, and he wasn't about to start. Lonnie's blues was a civilized thing, the guitar backing rich with complex jazz harmonies and intricate picking. Even today it's not for every blues fan...but his songs rarely fail to be meaningful, and there's never, ever been a better acoustic blues guitar technician. And let us not forget, he was a major influence on Robert Johnson (no relation).

◆

The first country blues hero on records was a 300-pound blind street singer from Texas with the unforgettable name of **Blind Lemon Jefferson**. It was Paramount Records, the most committed to black music of all the labels, that took the plunge with Blind Lemon early in 1926.

Blind Lemon grew up in Wortham, Texas, a town of 1000 some 65 miles south of Dallas. The year 1897 is often given as his birthdate, but he was probably born a few years earlier. "Lemon" came from his light complexion; the word "Blind" was commonly tacked on to the name of any sightless entertainer in the 1920s. Like so many other blind musicians, Lemon sang and played on street corners for spare change, and also played for picnics and house parties. Being better than most, he managed to make a living doing this, especially after he moved to Dallas around 1917.

Blind Lemon soon found he could make even more money by taking his act on the road. He sang and played all over the South, amazing everyone with his high, clear, powerful voice and his fancy guitar licks. Aspiring young pickers eagerly volunteered to guide him around. The media may not have noticed—they didn't care about street singers—but word of mouth had made Jefferson a celebrity on the plantations and in the small towns...which is to say there was at least a fair-sized ready-made market for his first records.

"Long Lonesome Blues," "That Black Snake Moan," and "Rabbit Foot Blues" were all big sellers. So was "Jack O' Diamond Blues," which is as close to a "field holler" as anything recorded in the 1920s, with a rare bottleneck turn by Jefferson.

Blind Lemon is unusual among acoustic bluesmen in that most of his music was not meant for dancing, but for listening. Typically, he sang each line in free rhythm, then answered it with his guitar. Most of his songs used the traditional three-line blues stanza, but they rarely came out to exactly 12 bars! Both the vocal line and the guitar response would go on as long as they wanted to. Small wonder that nobody could accompany Lemon; nearly all his records are solos. He did record enough dance pieces to show he could more than hold his own, though, along with a few pieces that recall early "songster" blues ("One Dime Blues").

Lemon recorded about 90 sides for Paramount, including a few religious songs under the name of Deacon L.J. Bates, and eight for OKeh (only two of these were released. Too bad—the OKeh sound is much better!). Most of his best work was done in 1926 and 1927. On his later records the lyrics tended to be less interesting, the guitar work less energetic and inventive. It was as if he was obliged to keep on making new records after he'd used up all his best stuff, and just wasn't able to come up with new stuff of similar quality. That was to happen again and again with blues singers in the next couple of decades. He died in December 1929; a persistent legend says he froze to death in a Chicago

BLIND LEMON JEFFERSON

KING OF THE COUNTRY BLUES

(Yazoo 1069)
Overall song selection, sound restoration, and provocative liner notes make this the best of numerous Jefferson CD reissues, though it omits important early "hits" like "Jack O' Diamond Blues" (perhaps not even Yazoo could clean up the sound to its satisfaction).

snowstorm. No death certificate has ever been found.

Considering his fame, Lemon had few successful imitators. His gifts were so unusual that many simply gave up the effort. One song of his that has remained a standard is "Match Box Blues." There's also the deeply moving "See That My Grave Is Kept Clean" (a.k.a. "One Kind Favor"), which Lemon recorded in his less exhibitionistic "songster" mode.

BLIND BLAKE

RAGTIME GUITAR'S FOREMOST FINGERPICKER

(Yazoo 1068)
Like Yazoo's Blind Lemon set, this omits a few early breakthrough hits, but it's otherwise totally wonderful. If one CD isn't enough, Document Records has four CDs of Blake's more or less complete works.

Blind Lemon was king of the blues in the 1920s, and his best records are still amazing today, despite that awful Paramount sound.

A few months after signing Blind Lemon, Paramount made another major find. **Blind Blake** (18??-19??) is about as different from Blind Lemon as can be. Only a passable singer, he was the finest, most booty-shakin' dance musician that acoustic blues ever knew. Whereas Lemon calls to mind lonesome street corners and big wide Texas spaces, Blind Blake is gin mills, smoky speakeasies, hot bodies.

At least it seems like he played in gin mills and smoky speakeasies. Actually, we know next to nothing about his life. He was probably born in the 1890s and died in the 1930s, and may have been from Florida. He hung around Chicago long enough to make about 85 sides on his own, along with guitar accompaniments for several other singers including Ma Rainey, and a few precious collaborations with jazzmen like Johnny Dodds. At any tempo, Blake's beat is irresistible, his guitar fingerpicking astounding. (Ry Cooder was among the first revivalists to pick up on it.)

Blind Willie McTell (1901-1959) was born in rural Georgia and spent most of his life in Atlanta. Like other Atlanta players, McTell specialized in twelve-string guitar, the same instrument Lead Belly later made famous. He sang in a distinctive tenor croon, a little like Lonnie Johnson's but not as refined. Despite never selling a lot of records, he made a large number for various labels between 1927 and 1956. Two sessions made for folksong collectors in 1940 and 1956 revealed his considerable non-blues repertoire. The commercial recordings, as one would expect, are mostly blues. One of them, "Statesboro Blues" (1928), became a great blues-revival favorite after it appeared on the first worthwhile rural blues LP compilation, the one accompanying Samuel Chartets' 1959 book *The Country Blues*. It became a concert mainstay for Taj Mahal and ultimately The Allman Brothers.

Another Atlanta twelve-string picker was Robert Hicks, known on records as **Barbecue Bob** (1902-1931). Unlike McTell, Bob sold lots of records; he was Columbia's #1 rural blues artist of the 1920s. A more limited guitarist than McTell, he did a few things very well, all of them superbly recorded by Columbia's skilled engineers. "Yo Yo Blues" is a splendid fast bottleneck piece, frequently imitated by others; "Mississippi Heavy Water Blues" is another tribute to the horrific floods of 1927 that inspired Bessie Smith's "Back Water Blues." He died of a lung infection at age 29. Robert's brother also made records in a similar vein, under the name **Charlie Lincoln**; his "Jealous Hearted Blues" was a good seller.

♦

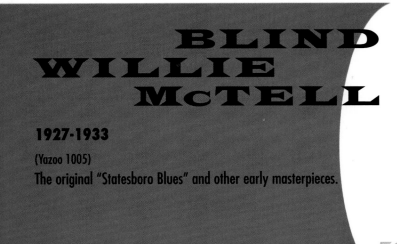

BLIND WILLIE McTELL

1927-1933

(Yazoo 1005)

The original "Statesboro Blues" and other early masterpieces.

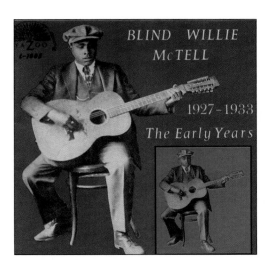

BLIND WILLIE McTELL

1927-1933
The Early Years

Most blues fans today would vote for the Mississippi Delta—the flat cotton country of northwest Mississippi, around Clarksdale, south of Memphis—as the Motherlode of guitar blues.* In the 1920s, when future heroes Robert Johnson and Muddy Waters were kids, Son House and Tommy Johnson were tearing up the country jook joints, along with the man who would latter be dubbed "The father of Delta blues," Charlie Patton.

Record companies in the mid-1920s knew nothing about any of that. The Delta was off the beaten path, and none of its singers had made a name for himself elsewhere like Blind Lemon had. Eventually, though, the Delta began to yield up its treasures.

Tommy Johnson (1896-1956) was the first of Patton's circle to record. Victor Records, the industry's sales leader and predecessor to RCA, captured "Big Road Blues" and three other songs in Memphis in February, 1928, and four more blues in August.

Born in southern Mississippi, Johnson moved to the Delta in his teens and came under Patton's spell. Later he moved to Jackson, where he continued to sing and play into the 1950s.

Tommy did like his liquor; when he couldn't get any, he was known to ingest Sterno "canned heat" for the alcohol it contained. He recorded a blues about it, after which the 1960s blues band Canned Heat was named. He sang in a rich voice with more tremolo than most, breaking into an eerie falsetto now and then. The word is that his records are only a shadow of the almost crazed live show he put on in his prime. He used to tell people he got his talent by selling his soul to the Devil, years before people began saying the same thing about Robert Johnson (no relation, as far as we know).

Tommy's "Big Road Blues" was a minor regional hit, and the word got back to **Charlie Patton** (1891-1934), who taught him the song. Charlie had heard

---

*The Delta was originally a vast swamp, rich in white-oak timber. During the 1890s, it was drained and cleared. Protected by the new Mississippi levee, it became cotton country. The recent invention of the cotton gin had made cotton a profitable crop, but it was still labor-intensive. See page 58.

BARBECUE BOB

CHOCOLATE TO THE BONE

(Yazoo 2005)

CANNED HEAT BLUES

MASTERS OF THE DELTA BLUES

(Bluebird 60147)

Features Tommy Johnson along with songs by Ishman Bracey (another Delta singer who recorded his brooding blues at the same sessions as Johnson) and some fine tracks by Memphis songster Furry Lewis.

about a Jackson merchant named H. C. Spier, who was also a free-lance record company talent scout. He had someone write Spier a letter about him (Patton was illiterate). Spier went to Patton's home to hear him, was suitably impressed by his vitality and the large number of songs he knew, and recommended him to Paramount Records. Paramount reportedly considered him the label's best find since Blind Lemon. They recorded and released 42 Patton songs within less than a year. At first they sold fairly well locally—it seems "Pony Blues" sold around 50,000—but there are only a handful of surviving copies of Patton's later releases.

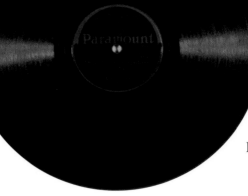

No matter…nearly all of them are available on CD today. The Paramounts reveal an utterly uninhibited performer, with prodigious energy, a brutal vocal attack, and a violent beat. Even with the low-budget sound (Paramount's recording had improved a bit, but not that much) Charlie is totally in your face. Charlie Patton's records were the first blues records you can truly call *heavy*, belying his small stature (5'7", 135 lbs).

Charlie learned his music growing up on Dockery's cotton plantation in Sunflower County, the heart of the Delta. The people he learned from are just shadowy names today—Henry Sloan, Earl Harris, D. Irvin. Patton was to live at Dockery's most of his life, entertaining the plantation's hundreds of African-American tenant farmers and their neighbors, at least when he hadn't been banned from the place for rowdy behavior. He doesn't seem to have travelled outside Mississippi and Arkansas, except for his recording sessions. The last of these was in New York, less than three months before his death of heart disease at age 43. Though some of the fire is gone, these 1934 sessions are still fine blues.

By general consensus, Charlie Patton gets the lion's share of the credit for making the Delta blues the snarling beast that it is, the most energetic and intense of all the infinite variations of blues. Robert Johnson, Muddy Waters, Elmore James, even Jimi Hendrix—and everyone who's ever played or enjoyed any of their music—are in Charlie's debt as well.

◆

Son House (1902-1988) was the next great Delta bluesman to emerge. Recruited for Paramount by H.C. Spier, the same man who found Patton, he travelled with Patton to the latter's final Paramount session in Grafton, Wis., in May 1930, and recorded ten sides himself. Paramount was fading fast by that time, and sales were negligible...but House was one of the Delta's most popular live acts through the 1930s. He was the most readily identifiable single influence on both Robert Johnson, who recorded covers of his songs, and on Muddy Waters.

Born and raised in the Delta, House studied to be a preacher until the blues tempted him away in the 1920s. He was to be severely torn by conflict between the church and "the devil's music"

CHARLIE PATTON

FOUNDER OF THE DELTA BLUES

(Yazoo 1020)

KING OF THE DELTA BLUES

(Yazoo 2001)

Between them, these two CDs have all but a few of Patton's existing recordings.

Book: The Life and Music of CHARLIE PATTON: KING OF THE DELTA BLUES by Stephen Calt and Gayle Wardlow

(Rock Chapel Press)

About as definitive a biography of Patton as we're likely to see, exhaustively researched in Mississippi while many of Patton's contemporaries were still alive (1965-72).

throughout his life, no doubt contributing to his alcoholism and his rather somber personality—a total contrast to the crackup Charlie Patton. One of his greatest songs, "Preachin' the Blues" (covered by Robert Johnson), dealt directly with how the conflict affected him.

His music was also more somber than Patton's, and it probably struck people in the 1930s as being a little more modern, with its even, steady dance beat, its precise arrangements, and carefully controlled bottleneck technique. Yet Son House was second to none in the passion he put into his singing.

SON HOUSE

FATHER OF THE DELTA BLUES: THE COMPLETE 1965 SESSIONS

(Columbia 48867)
The comeback album, with Alan Wilson on backup guitar.

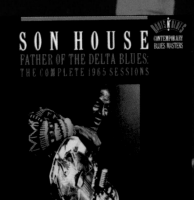

SON HOUSE
FATHER OF THE DELTA BLUES:
THE COMPLETE 1965 SESSIONS
CONTEMPORARY BLUES MASTERS

BO CARTER

BANANA IN YOUR FRUIT BASKET

(Yazoo 1064)

After making some fine recordings for Alan Lomax and the Library of Congress in the Delta in 1942, House left the Delta behind and moved to Rochester, N.Y., giving up music and living there in utter obscurity before blues enthusiasts tracked him down in 1964. In a nice twist of music history, a young white blues enthusiast named Alan Wilson, who had painstakingly learned House's guitar style from his old records, helped House relearn his own music which he hadn't played for years. Wilson later co-founded Canned Heat; House played folk festivals and coffeehouses until his health declined in the 1970s.

The Delta was of course not the only place in Mississippi where fabulous blues was made. One of the last artists to be signed by Paramount before it folded was the unclassifi-

able but incredible **Skip James** (1902-1969). James was from Bentonia, Miss., a little place not far from Jackson which seems to have had its own distinct style of musicmaking.

Like Blind Lemon Jefferson's, James' music was for listening more than for dancing…dark, doom-laden lyrics and melodies punctuated by dazzling guitar breaks (or, on a few sides, his eccentric piano playing). His original "I'm So Glad" (covered by Cream with Eric Clapton) is a spectacular example. (In the 1980s that same combination of exhilarating

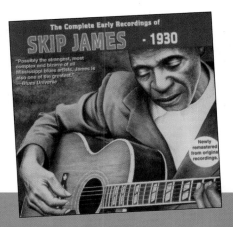

THE COMPLETE EARLY RECORDINGS OF

SKIP JAMES

(Yazoo 2009)

The sound restoration on these fabulously rare, often battered 78s is near-miraculous, but you still need to be tolerant of record scratch when you hear this. His 1960s recordings, less energetic but hauntingly beautiful, are on Vanguard CDs.

THE MISSISSIPPI SHEIKS

STOP AND LISTEN

(Yazoo 2006)

After the Paramount session, James sang spirituals for awhile but mostly worked outside music until his 1964 "rediscovery" led to a brief revival career.

✦

One Mississippian who had much better luck with the record industry in the early 1930s was Bo Chatmon (1893-1964), usually called **Bo Carter**. A blind singer-guitarist from the Jackson area, Bo is remembered as a fellow who didn't get into trouble. He was a teetotaler, almost unheard of for a bluesman in those days. But what an imagination! Bo came up with some of the bawdiest blues of that or any other era. "Banana In Your Fruit Basket," "Ram Rod Daddy," and "Please Warm My Wiener" were a few of his hits. Yazoo has released several compilations of his work; it's not the greatest blues ever recorded but its continuing appeal is undeniable! He was also the first to record the familiar "Corrine Corrina."

Bo Chatmon was also an intermittent member of **The Mississippi Sheiks**, a fiddle-and-guitar band which also featured his brothers Lonnie and Sam and their friend Walter Vincson (sometimes called Walter Jacobs, but no relation to 1950s Chicago harp wizard Little Walter Jacobs). The Sheiks did much of their live performing for white audiences, and knew plenty of pop songs and country fiddle tunes, a few of which they recorded—but their 80 released sides are mostly blues. Their biggest hit, "Sittin' On Top Of The

music and depressing messages would become standard for alternative rockers like Depeche Mode.) Robert Johnson did a guitar arrangement of one of James' piano pieces, "22-20 Blues" ("32-20" in Johnson's version).

World" (1930) is still a standard, memorably revived in 1957 by Howlin' Wolf. Another Sheiks success was "Stop And Listen Blues," based on the same unforgettable guitar riff as Tommy Johnson's "Big Road Blues."

✦

We will return to Mississippi, and meet the immortal Robert Johnson, a few pages down the road. It's time to catch up on what was happening elsewhere in the late 1920s and early 1930s, including a new brand of blues which became nationally popular very quickly, far more so (at least for the moment) than anything from the Delta.

VARIOUS ARTISTS

MASTERS OF THE DELTA BLUES

(Yazoo 2002)
This compilation has all of House's surviving Paramounts plus tracks by Tommy Johnson, Bukka White and other Delta stalwarts.

MISSISSIPPI MASTERS: EARLY AMERICAN BLUES CLASSICS 1927–35

(Yazoo 2007)
In the 1920s, as in later times, there were fine singers who got to make just one or two single records, then disappeared without a trace. William Harris, Otto Virgial, Geeshie Wiley, Blind Joe Reynolds, Elvie Thomas, King Solomon Hill and Garfield Akers never gained fame or fortune from their music, but this entire CD is a knockout with some of the hardest, hottest acoustic blues ever sung and played by anyone. The female singers — a rarity for country blues — are perhaps the finest of all.

Sharecropping

You will often read that such-and-such a blues singer was a sharecropper, or that his parents were share-croppers. In the early 20th century, most African-Americans in the rural South were sharecroppers.

Sharecropping worked like this: the big planta-tions were divided into plots of two or three dozen acres. Each of these plots would be farmed by a black family, which would be provided a house (shack was more like it) and the use of the plantation-owned school and church (and, sometimes, the plantation-owned jook joint). In lieu of rent, the plantation own-ers had a right to a share (typically half) of the crop.

It seems fair enough...but since the plantation owned everything, and the sharecroppers (tenants) were generally illiterate and powerless, plantation owners rarely resisted the temptation to abuse the sys-tem, and their tenants. When the price of cotton tum-bled after World War I, there wasn't enough money to go around anymore, and guess who got left out.

Sharecroppers stayed on the plantation because they had nowhere else to go. In the 1940s, all that changed quite radically; see "Blues On the Move".

The Doctor Said, "Give Him Jug Band Music!"

Jug band music was prescribed as a cure for whatever ails you in a 1966 song by The Lovin' Spoonful. Forty years earlier, jug band music was a familiar sound on the streets of Memphis and other Southern cities. It might have been the first "retro" blues; we get the feeling that even in the 1920s it brought nostalgic memories of old times down home.

A jug band consists of a harmonica and/or kazoo and/or violin, a guitar and/or banjo and/or man-dolin, and of course a jug—any large container with a smaller opening, which produces a deep bass sound when one blows across the opening (the bigger the jug, the deeper the sound). There were some who could play distinct bass notes on a jug, though a non-tonal "oomph" was more usual.

Jug bands tried to imitate the sound of a brass band, but the cheap portable instruments have an undeniable charm of their own. They played dance instrumentals (from hot jazz tunes to waltzes), folk songs from the songster repertoire, turn-of-the-cen-

THE MEMPHIS JUG BAND
(Yazoo 1067)

tury pop tunes and of course blues, which the record companies preferred.

There are accounts of jug bands playing in Louisville before 1910 and the style may have started there. It was in Memphis that the record companies found the best jug bands. The top jug band on records was the **Memphis Jug Band**, which consisted of singer-guitarist-harmonica player **Will Shade** (1898-1966) and whoever he happened to recruit for a particular performance in a local park or in a Beale Street brothel or gambling hall, or for a recording session. Frequent accomplices included singer-guitarist Will Weldon (who became a record star in the 1930s as "Casey Bill"), singer-kazooist Ben Ramey, and later on the virtuoso juggist Jab Jones. Their big rivals were **Cannon's Jug Stompers** led by veteran songster-banjoist-juggist **Gus Cannon** (1883-1979) and featuring Noah Lewis's fine harmonica.

The jug band "craze," such as it was, was pretty much over by 1930 (there was one terrific 1934 record session by the Memphis Jug Band). When

people began seriously collecting old blues 78s in the 1950s and '60s, however, jug band records shot to the top of many want lists. A

CANNON'S JUG STOMPERS
(Yazoo 1082/3)

folksinging group called The Rooftop Singers heard Cannon's Jug Stompers' 1929 record of "Walk Right In" and had a #1 pop hit with their own version. Young white musicians loved that raggedy, informal sound and formed jug bands of their own. The Jim Kweskin Jug Band made several wonderful LPs (some with Maria Muldaur, nee Maria D'Amato, on vocals). Canned Heat began as a jug band before switching to electric blues. An early version of the Grateful Dead was called Mother McCree's Uptown Jug Champions; Gus Cannon's "Viola Lee Blues" was on the Dead's first LP.

A Lot of Hokum

In 1928 Tampa Red and Georgia Tom recorded a lively, mildly risqué dance blues called "It's Tight Like That" for Vocalion Records. It was a smash, probably the best-selling non-vaudeville blues disc of the entire decade. Naturally, they soon recorded "It's Tight Like That No. 2" for Vocalion, but that wasn't all. They also went across the street and recorded a *very* similar song for Paramount, which called them "The Hokum Boys."

It soon developed that other musicians could imitate "It's Tight Like That" quite nicely too. Blind Blake was drafted for one session. Other record companies joined in with other "Hokum Boys" efforts. Eventually Big Bill Broonzy, just beginning his career, became the #1 Hokum Boy, often paired with the original Georgia Tom. They were labelled as the *Famous* Hokum Boys, just so you'd know. Well into the 1930s, they were still in that "Tight Like That" bag—fast blues with piano and guitar, risqué lyrics (more so as time went on), with the first line of the

12-bar blues chorus almost always divided into two or four short lines.

Tampa Red, who bailed out of the "hokum" craze early on, went on to a long and successful career as a fairly orthodox bluesman…as did Big Bill. Georgia Tom milked hokum for all it was worth until 1932, when he got religion. As Thomas Dorsey, he became the preeminent songwriter in African-American church music ("Peace In the Valley," "Precious Lord") and a prime innovator of the new style called gospel, having come a long way indeed from such hokum hits as "Selling That Stuff" and "Papa's Getting Hot."

The original "Tight Like That" can be found on MCA's *Blues Classics* box set (MCA 11441). In general, hokum has gotten little attention from reissue compilers, who assume listeners today would prefer more serious blues like Charlie Patton…who didn't sell anywhere near as many 78s in his day as the Hokum Boys did.

Thomas Georgia Dorsey and his Female Quartet, 1934

We aren't attempting to cover African-American religious music in this book—gospel could easily fill a book like this on its own—but anyone who enjoys the music described in these chapters should not miss **Blind Willie Johnson** (?1902-?1947). He was a street singer and slide guitarist who lived and worked in Dallas in the 1920s; his popularity rivalled Blind Lemon Jefferson's. He may have also sung blues, but if he recorded any, the masters have disappeared. He sang his Christian songs with the fury of a Charlie Patton. He played guitar with the percussive attack and stomping beat of a Delta bluesman, but with much more emphasis on the melody line. On his most famous

Boom or Bust

The early 1920s, the heyday of vaudeville blues on records, were boom times for the record industry in general. The reproduction that sounds so primitive today was miraculous and wonderful in those days. Even though single records cost close to $10 in today's money, people snapped them up by the millions.

Then along came radio. At first a squeaky plaything for hobbyists, it quickly became much more popular as sound quality improved. Radios didn't have to be wound up, and didn't need needles. Best of all, you could hear the latest song hits for free! In living rooms across America, phonographs were cast aside to make way for radios.

The Great Depression of the early 1930s nearly wiped out the record business. In 1933, only a grand

Holy Blues

recording, "Dark Was The Night—Cold Was The Ground," he dispenses with the words of the old hymn and moans the melody (with variations) in unison with his guitar. The effect is so awe-inspiring that when the record finishes, you may not want to put on another one for a while—just let it sink in.

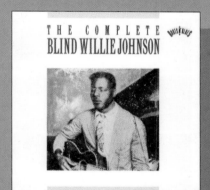

THE COMPLETE BLIND WILLIE JOHNSON

(Columbia 52835)
We are most fortunate that Columbia recorded Johnson fairly copiously (his records did outsell those of most bluesmen in the 1920s) and with what was, for the time, excellent sound quality.

total of six million single records were sold in the USA. (Many individual CDs today sell more copies than that).

In the late 1930s records made a comeback, helped by better times and lower prices. By 1935, the three major record companies were releasing virtually all their blues on labels which sold for 35¢ per single, versus 75¢ in the 1920s. Another factor was the end of Prohibition. With beer legalized, taverns opened by the tens of thousands, and nearly all of them had jukeboxes. Many records of the mid- and late-1930s, including blues records, were made primarily with jukeboxes in mind.

Chapter 4
The New Urban
Blues

Things that make us think of a blues performance as "urban":

- A terse, understated style of singing (compared to the dramatics of vaudeville blues and the more intense emotionalism of Delta singers).
- Piano accompaniment, with or without guitar or other instruments. (There were several excellent urban blues guitarists, but piano dominates the idiom.)
- The accompaniment is simplified, with lots of repeated patterns, less elaborate improvisation.
- Standard 12-bar (occasionally 8-bar) choruses, with little deviation.
- A strong, steady beat for dancing.

Urban blues was played live in "barrelhouses" (a loose term for inelegant drinking establishments, legal or otherwise), brothels, and also in theatres. We don't know exactly how or where the urban blues started, any more than we can pinpoint the origin of rural blues. We have to assume it had been around for awhile before 1928, because after Leroy Carr made the first urban blues hit record that year, numerous other fine singer-pianists made their debuts in short order.

Within a couple of years of its disc debut, urban blues accounted for the majority of the "race" records sold in America. It was the basis for the music that would dominate blues right into the 1950s.

Leroy Carr (1905-1935) made that first hit record, "How Long How Long Blues," and many more in his short career. Other standards he introduced include "In The Evening When The Sun Goes Down," "Sloppy Drunk," "Prison Bound," and "Blues Before Sunrise."

He was born in Nashville but grew up in Indianapolis, and lived there until his death. His repertoire wasn't limited to blues; his recordings also include a delightful kids' song about life behind the scenes at the circus ("Carried Water For The Elephant") and his heartfelt crooning of Irving Berlin's "How About Me." In 1929 he recorded "Straight Alky Blues"; six years later he was dead of acute alcoholism, a month past his thirtieth birthday.

No small part of Carr's success was due to his performing partner, guitarist **Scrapper Blackwell** (1903-1962). Blackwell (who sometimes sang along with Carr on uptempo songs) was a skilled all-around guitarist, as shown by some solo records he made. He had a very special approach for playing with Carr, though. He played stinging single-string counter-melodies between Carr's vocal lines. It was one way of making an acoustic guitar heard above a piano. Scrapper's work with Carr was the genesis of blues lead guitar—the guitar as a solo instrument, not responsible for the rhythm as it was in rural blues.

One of Carr's most effective competitors in the urban piano blues arena was William Bunch, better known as **Peetie Wheatstraw** (1902-1941). Born in Tennessee, he arrived in East St. Louis, Illinois, in 1929 and quickly became a regular on the lively St. Louis blues scene. He began recording in 1930 and had a new record out almost every month from 1934 until his death at 39 in an auto accident.

Unlike other bluesmen who agonized about doing the devil's music, Peetie made no bones about it: he was often billed on record labels as "The High Sheriff From Hell" or "The Devil's Son-In-Law." He was a more outgoing singer than Carr, with a deep, lusty baritone voice, and also a fine blues poet—though he didn't always have enough good lyrical ideas to fill all the records he was asked to make, and

It apparently wasn't easy to keep the team together. Scrapper, whose nickname accurately reflected his ornery personality (he died in an alley brawl at age 59), resented the spotlight that fell on his tall, handsome, affable partner. However, Scrapper does his thing on all but eight of Carr's more than 100 recordings.

LEROY CARR

HURRY DOWN SUNSHINE:
THE ESSENTIAL RECORDINGS OF LEROY CARR

(Indigo [UK] 2016)

Roosevelt Sykes

sometimes resorted to random verses recycled from other blues. A succession of fine guitarists—Lonnie Johnson and Charley Jordan from St. Louis, Casey Bill and Kokomo Arnold from other places—played Scrapper to Peetie's Leroy.

Another St. Louis singer-pianist of the 1930s was **Walter Davis** (1912-1963). A favorite of all-powerful record producer Lester Melrose, he made over 150 recordings. Some are terrific, others uninspired. On the best ones, his mournful voice and simple but distinctive piano style are deeply moving. His "Come Back Baby" became a standard, and the rowdy, leering "I Can Tell By The Way You Smell" belongs in any collection of blues erotica.

Roosevelt Sykes (1906-1984) was yet another St. Louis piano blues pioneer, whose career lasted the longest of all. His style was rootsier than Leroy Carr's, and more elaborate; he didn't need a guitarist to keep things interesting. His first hit, "44 Blues" (1929), is a barrelhouse piece that has more in common rhythmically and thematically with the Delta guitar blues of Charlie Patton and Son House than it does with Carr, but Sykes eventually settled into the contemporary urban groove. Like Wheatstraw he had a new single out almost every month in the late 1930s. Along with hits like "Night Time Is The Right Time" (an appealing knockoff of Carr's "In The Evening When The Sun Goes Down"), he came up with such colorful items as "Journey From The Germs" and "Hospital, Heaven Or Hell." He moved to Chicago in the 1940s and was a big part of that city's blues scene until he felt his traditional style crowded out by the electric sounds of the 1950s. He then found a more congenial home in New Orleans, working steadily there and around the world until his death at 78.

Eurreal **"Little Brother" Montgomery** (1906-1985) was a versatile pianist from the Louisiana backwoods who played jazz and pop songs as well as blues. He appears to have originated one of the most famous early piano blues pieces, which he called "Vicksburg Blues" (later it became better known as "44," as in firearm). He adapted better than most to changing times: he played splendidly on several highly electric late 1950s sessions by Otis Rush and Magic Sam, and continued to record well into his seventies.

The first urban blues guitar player to make a splash was Hudson Woodbridge, a.k.a. Hudson Whittaker (1904-1981), much better known as **Tampa Red.** Like Leroy Carr he unleashed a monster with his first release on the Vocalion label. "It's Tight Like

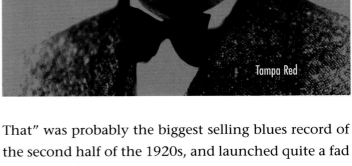

Tampa Red

That" was probably the biggest selling blues record of the second half of the 1920s, and launched quite a fad for what came to be called "hokum" blues (see p. 60).

Tampa Red soon left "hokum" to others and settled into his own thing. His music fits comfortably into the urban blues category, with its regular structure, prominent dance beat, and restrained singing.

He usually worked with a pianist, but had no trouble making his guitar heard. It was a National with a self-contained resonator to boost the sound, a model popularized by the Hawaiian guitarists who were so popular on the mainland early in the 20th century. Indeed, one can detect a bit of Hawaiian influence in his playing. A self-taught musician, he played with a bottleneck (see p. 77)

LITTLE BROTHER MONTGOMERY

COMPLETE RECORDED WORKS 1930-1936 IN CHRONOLOGICAL ORDER

(Document 5109)

with which he got a sliding, glissando effect on the top strings. Bottlenecks were also used by rural blues guitarists all over the South...but Tampa Red's playing stood out from the rest due to his sweet tone and careful intonation (getting all the pitches, the microtones just right). For pure precision, Lonnie Johnson was his only peer in those days. Small wonder Vocalion billed Tampa Red as "The Guitar Wizard," and recorded several instrumental guitar solos by him along with vocal blues. In the early 1930s he added a kazoo to his act, held with a neck brace and played simultaneously with the guitar. He often used this on the good-timey pop-flavored tunes he played for variety, but he could also snarl out a mean blues line on kazoo.

In all, Tampa Red had over 150 78 rpm singles released in his career, probably more than any other blues artist. These included such standards-to-be as "Mean Mistreater" (revived by Muddy Waters), "Black Angel Blues" (the source for B.B. King's "Sweet Little Angel"), and "When Things Go Wrong With You" (which became Elmore James' "It Hurts Me Too"). In the 1930s his Chicago home became a major hangout for visiting blues singers, many of whom he helped get recording deals.

TAMPA RED

THE BLUEBIRD RECORDINGS, 1934-1936

(RCA Bluebird 07863 66721-2)
This is the first volume in what will hopefully be a complete set of his works from 1934 to 1953.

TAMPA RED THE GUITAR WIZARD

(Columbia 53235)

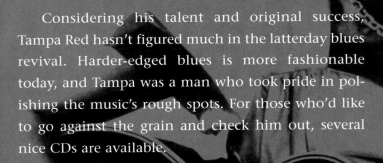

Considering his talent and original success, Tampa Red hasn't figured much in the latterday blues revival. Harder-edged blues is more fashionable today, and Tampa was a man who took pride in polishing the music's rough spots. For those who'd like to go against the grain and check him out, several nice CDs are available.

The blues of the late 1920s and 1930s was almost as firmly dominated by men as vaudeville blues had been by women. The greatest exception to all that testosterone was **Memphis Minnie** (1897-1973). Born Lizzie Douglas in Louisiana, she moved with her family as a child to a farm near Walls, Mississippi, just over the state line from Memphis. An unruly girl, she ran away from home often, often to Memphis' Beale Street, where she started singing and playing guitar as a teenager (known as Kid Douglas) and learned to duke it out with the men—she would always be known as a woman not to be messed with. It was there she joined up with singer-guitarist Joe McCoy. A Columbia Records man heard them singing in a Beale Street barbershop and sent them to New York for a 1929 record session. It was apparently someone at Columbia who named them "Kansas Joe and Memphis Minnie."

The Columbia sides feature excellent guitar and rather nervous, tentative singing. They didn't sell much. (Decades later, "When The Levee Breaks" inspired a famous Led Zeppelin album track.) Things were different when the pair recorded in Memphis eight months later, for Vocalion. Minnie, top billed this time, took one of the Columbia flops, slowed it down just a bit, got comfortable with the microphone, and delivered a masterpiece—"Bumble Bee." Though it was all guitars, "Bumble Bee" had a lot in common with the new urban blues—the slowish tempo, the regular 12-bar choruses with repeated, catchy guitar hooks, the delivery that eschewed the

And whatever became of "Kansas Joe" McCoy? After he and Minnie split up, he formed a Chicago-based jazz band called the Harlem Hamfats, which had a few hits in the mid-1930s featuring Joe's bluesy vocals. One of the Hamfats' songs, "Weed Smoker's Dream," evolved into the 1940s blues-pop crossover hit "Why Don't You Do Right," the song that made a star of pop singer Peggy Lee.

If there was any guitarist in the new urban blues who could match Memphis Minnie lick for lick, it

big drama of a Bessie Smith for a plainer sort of emotional communication.

Memphis Minnie is often classed as a country blues person, presumably because she played guitar...but she really was an urban blues guitarist, more than holding her own with all those male urban blues pianists. She was to remain one of the half-dozen most popular blues artists in America until World War II, with her biggest hit coming in 1941—"Me And My Chauffeur." Her original lyrics are among the most interesting in all of blues. They are intensively analyzed, along with her unique personality and career, in an absorbing biography by Paul and Beth Garon, *Woman With Guitar: Memphis Minnie's Blues.*

MEMPHIS MINNIE

HOODOO LADY (1933–1937)
(COLUMBIA 46775)

was **Big Bill Broonzy** (1893-1958). Big Bill is often hailed as the great connection between country and city blues. Raised in rural Mississippi and Arkansas, his first instrument was the fiddle, which he played at dances for neighboring whites. After serving in World War I, he moved to Chicago in 1920. Switching to guitar, he soon got a reputation as one of the city's best pickers and singers. Record companies drafted him to carry on the "hokum" craze started by Tampa Red, but he soon became better known for his original songs in a more mainstream blues mode, usually recorded with piano alongside his guitar, sometimes with horns and/or bass and drums. He was a fine, big-voiced singer and an imaginative, crafty songwriter. Even new single every month in the late 1930s was above average. And he was the consummate urban blues guitarist; there was nobody better at creating those regular, repeated patterns that made dancers feel right at home, and nobody save Scrapper Blackwell who was better at working with pianists.

By the time Leroy Carr died in 1935, Big Bill was ready to take his place as the country's top "race" recording artist, which he pretty much was until World War II. Despite his success, he continued working in factories for most of this period. Unlike many bluesman, Big Bill put a premium on stability in his lifestyle, and a regular paycheck was a high priority in the days when "race" artists earned little or no royalties for either their records or their songs.

In 1938, meanwhile, record producer/concert promoter John Hammond was looking for someone to fill the slot he'd set aside for the recently murdered Robert Johnson in an elaborate Carnegie Hall presentation called "Spirituals to Swing," designed to showcase the entire spectrum of African-American music. Hammond called on Big Bill, who sang two of his hits with boogie pianist Albert Ammons and Count Basie's

BIG BILL BROONZY

THE YOUNG BIG BILL BROONZY

(Yazoo 1011)

A fine showcase for Broonzy's guitar work, from before the time of his greatest success.

GOOD TIME TONIGHT

(Columbia 46219)

Tough, swinging combo blues from the peak of his popularity in the late 1930s.

rhythm section. Though that didn't change Bill's career much for the moment, it laid the groundwork for what Bill did after his "race" record career waned in the 1940s. He remade himself in the image of Lead Belly and Josh White and became a "folk bluesman" singing for almost exclusively white audiences. He had considerable success at this, mainly in Europe, and became the first bluesman to write his autobiography (*Big Bill's Blues*, with Yannick Bruynoghe—1955).

Alan Lomax, who interviewed Broonzy extensively, devotes a revealing chapter to him in his book *The Land Where the Blues Began* (Pantheon, 1993).

Some of Big Bill's 1930s success rubbed off on his halfbrother, **Washboard Sam** (Robert Brown—1910-1966). Sam laid down an infectious dance beat on a real washboard, straight from the laundry, with various attachments bolted to it for special effects (including an old phonograph

his records, and brought along the same musicians heard on his own sides.

Moreover, Bill's and Sam's recording sessions were both supervised by the same man. As a matter of fact, so were the vast majority of the blues sessions on two of the three major blues record labels (Bluebird and Vocalion) from 1935 until after World War II. The man's name was **Lester Melrose** (1891-1968). He was a Chicago jazz fan and record retailer who got into producing records during the hokum craze (see p. 60). and never looked back. He built his little empire around Big Bill and Tampa Red, whom he knew from hokum. Bill and Tampa were both very good at seeking out new artists and getting them ready to record, and Melrose took full advantage of this.

Melrose was very much aware of the importance of the jukebox, and realized that records with a rhythm section came across better than records with just a guitar and/or piano. Later he often added a clarinet, a trumpet, and/or a saxophone or two. Not messing with success, he used the same musicians on session after session. The rollicking two-beat barrelhouse piano of "Black Bob" Hudson dominates most Melrose sessions until 1938. Then the more modern four-four of Joshua Altheimer took over until the latter's death in 1940 (at age 30, of pneumonia). He was succeeded by Blind John Davis, Memphis Slim, Champion Jack Dupree and Big Maceo.

turntable, which made a nice bell sound). He also sang, with a big voice much like Broonzy's if a little less expressive. For awhile he matched Broonzy hit for hit, working for a rival label. Actually, Big Bill wrote many of Sam's songs, backed him on most of

WASHBOARD SAM

ROCKIN' MY BLUES AWAY

(Bluebird 61042)

Good stuff, though a few more of his best-sellers might have made a more representative package.

MONEY BLUES

The latter three also became well known singers. **Memphis Slim** (Peter Chatman, 1915-1988) had a hit for Melrose with "Beer Drinking Woman" (1940) and more success after World War II when he became the most successful holdout for 1930s-style urban blues on the increasingly electrified Chicago scene. In 1955 his composition "Every Day I Have The Blues" became a huge hit for Count Basie's band featuring jazz singer Joe Williams. In 1962 Slim moved to Paris where he was hailed as a giant and treated like a celebrity; Europe was far ahead of the U.S.A. in giving older bluesmen the respect they deserved. **Champion Jack Dupree** (William Thomas Dupree, 1909-1992) had a remarkably similar career: a few sessions with Melrose in 1940-41, some hits in the mid-1950s on King Records (humorous blues like "She Cooks Me Cabbage" and "Me And My

Little Bill Gaither, Memphis Slim, and Big Bill Broonzy

Mule" were his specialty then) and celebrity in Europe for the last thirty-plus years of his life. **Big Maceo** Merriweather (1905-1953), a thunderous pianist, wrote and recorded the very popular "Worried Life Blues" in 1941; his career was cut short by a stroke in 1946.

Melrose had two other female stars besides Memphis Minnie, both named Lil. **Lil Johnson** had one of Melrose's first and biggest hits—a bawdy stomper called "Hot Nuts (Get 'Em From The Peanut Man)." After numerous followups flopped, she faded into utter obscurity. **Lil Green** (1919-1954) was a Big Bill Broonzy protege. At her first session, at age 20, she recorded Broonzy's song "Romance In The Dark" with a nice Big Bill guitar solo and Champion Jack Dupree on piano. This was an early (1940) example of a "blues ballad," a song with a blueslike melody but a

32-bar chorus like a pop ballad. This form would become tremendously popular after the war. Lil Green also did well with her version of "Why Don't You Do Right," the likely inspiration for the Benny Goodman/Peggy Lee megahit. She would die of pneumonia at only 34, in 1954.

Lester Melrose is the bane of some blues 78 collectors' existence. Those clarinet solos do get tiresome sometimes. But along with a steady flow of jukebox hits by Big Bill, Washboard Sam and Tampa Red, he also recorded many fine singers in more traditional settings, such as Bukka White, Tommy McClennan and Sonny Boy Williamson. We'll meet them in a few pages. First, though, it's time to get acquainted with a few extraordinary Southern bluesmen who had varying degrees of success outside the Melrose orbit in the 1930s.

Boogie Woogie

Although urban piano blues of the 1920s is often associated with slow to medium tempos, most of the pianists also played uptempo music for dancing. In 1928 a young Chicago singer-pianist (originally from Alabama) named Clarence **"Pine Top" Smith** (1904-1929) recorded a fast blues enlivened by his commands to the dancers, one of which was "boogie woogie!" Released as "Pine Top's Boogie Woogie," the record was a sizable hit. Alas, Pine Top didn't get to enjoy his celebrity for long; he died at age 25 a few months later after catching a wayward bullet in a bar room brawl.

The disc remained a favorite with dancers and musicians, both white and black. When jazz record collecting became established as a hobby in the 1930s, "Pine Top's Boogie Woogie" was quickly recognized as a prize item. Collectors searched for more like it, and soon discovered a much scarcer disc in similar style, "Honky Tonk Train Blues" by **Meade Lux Lewis** (1905-1964), recorded for Paramount in 1929. (Lewis and Smith had been good friends.)

By 1935 there were enough dedicated jazz collectors so that record companies started reissuing classics and making new records in older styles, especially for collectors. Guitar-centered blues was ignored, but fast instrumental piano blues was a major attraction, becoming generally known as "boogie woogie" in Pine Top's honor. Meade Lux Lewis re-recorded "Honky Tonk Train" that year. Another old pal of Lewis' and Smith's, Albert Ammons, made the first of his many records in 1936.

In 1938 Tommy Dorsey's big band had a hit with an instrumental version of Pine Top's "Boogie Woogie." That kicked off a real boogie woogie craze, resulting in a lot of club work and some best-selling records for Lewis, Ammons and also for **Pete Johnson** (1904-1967), who came to New York from Kansas City with legendary blues shouter Big Joe Turner.

The boogie woogie craze eventually went the way of all crazes, but not before adding "boogie" to the more or less permanent national vocabulary.

Bottleneck

Anyone seeking to play expressive blues guitar looks for a way to play "blue notes"—those notes, essential to blues singing, which fall between the notes of the conventional Western musical scale (see pages 14-15). Just as they fall between the keys of a piano, they fall between the frets of a guitar, which are intended to provide the conventional 12 notes of the scale.

The most common way to play blue notes is to "bend" the strings. By fretting a string in the normal manner, and then pushing the string to one side along the fret, thus increasing its tension, the pitch is raised enough to provide that blue note. By varying the distance the string is pushed, the guitarist can vary the pitch. Skillful blues guitarists can use this technique to subtly mimic the patterns of speech as well as song—B.B. King is a master of that.

Very early in the history of blues guitar, someone (probably in the Mississippi Delta) discovered another way to make blue notes and other pitch variations. This unknown hero placed the sawed-off neck of a bottle over the little finger of his left (fretting) hand. Our hero found that by moving this hard cylindrical object up and down the guitar neck, he could play any note of the scale and anything in between, regardless of the frets. The technique was doubtless inspired by Hawaiian "steel" guitar, in which the frets aren't used at all, and all notes are formed with a heavy steel bar pressed against the strings. With a bottleneck, though, the guitarist is free to use his remaining fingers to fret strings in the normal manner, and thus provide the bass patterns essential for a dance musician along with those expressive blue notes and slides. Robert Johnson was a master of that.

Early on, resourceful guitarists discovered that certain metal bushings (from an auto parts store) worked just as well as glass bottlenecks. You can make a bottleneck the old way today by carefully sawing off the neck of a bottle and then holding the sharp edge over a Bunsen burner to round it off. Make sure it's just the right size to fit snugly over your little finger (some guitarists use the fourth finger instead). Or you can buy a bottleneck in a music store, either glass or metal. (You can also buy harmonicas and mikes made especially for that Little Walter sound. We've come a long way.)

To bend or to bottleneck? Many guitarists do both, even in the same piece. The bottleneck produces a characteristic jangly sound, and also a distinctive clatter as it bumps over the frets. Some people find this noise distracting, others can't live without it. Moral: blues has a flavor for everyone's taste.

Chapter 5

More From the Hinterlands

Blind Boy Fuller (Fulton Allen, 1907-1941) was the most popular solo singer-guitarist on records in the late 1930s. Like Blind Blake before him, Fuller sang and played in the "Piedmont" style associated with the Southeast. More relaxed and lyrical than Blake (and a considerably better singer), Fuller was still a fine dance musician, and the archetypical Piedmont bluesman.

Piedmont blues features complex fingerpicking, relaxed singing and generally major tonalities. One associates it with a lighter touch than, say, Delta blues. It may be light, but it's not lightweight; Piedmont blues can be very profound and moving. Nobody sang it more movingly than Blind Boy Fuller.

Fuller spent most of his life in Durham, N.C. He learned some of his guitar from another Durham resident, the **Rev. Gary Davis** (1896-1972), who would go on to be a popular performer during the 1960s folk/blues revival. Fuller was discovered singing in front of a tobacco warehouse by a local record dealer, J. B. Long, who got him a record deal. From 1935 until his death at age 33 of a kidney ailment (perhaps due to alcoholism), Fuller produced 127 sides of uniformly fine blues. His standards include "Step It Up and Go" and "Truckin' My Blues Away."

Blind Boy Fuller

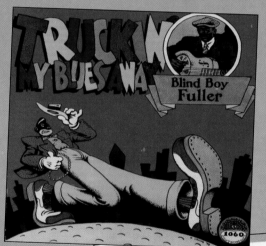

BLIND BOY FULLER

TRUCKIN' MY BLUES AWAY

(Yazoo 1060)

EAST COAST PIEDMONT STYLE

(Columbia 46777)

Each of these CDs is a fine selection of Fuller's most appealing work. His complete recordings have been reissued on six CDs on the Document label.

Brownie McGhee with Sticks McGhee

Fuller's chief disciple was **Brownie McGhee** (1915-1996) who began his recording career as "Blind Boy Fuller No. 2." McGhee and another Durhamite, harmonica player Sonny Terry, went on to form a highly successful duo after World War II.

Postwar success in the folk revival was also in the cards for another Piedmont picker, **Joshua White** (1914-1969). Starting in the late 1930s, White cleverly and skillfully reconfigured his music and his career for his new audience of highbrow Caucasians, who called him "Josh" and revered him as a great folksinger. Before that, however, he was a South Carolina country boy, who made his recording debut in 1932 at age 18. His earliest work is fairly "pure" Piedmont blues.

Decca Records, the only major label that didn't use Lester Melrose in the late 1930s, had two "country" guitar playing bluesmen who rivalled Fuller during that period, Kokomo Arnold and Sleepy John Estes.

Launched in 1934, Decca Records had its first blues hit that fall with "Milk Cow Blues" by **Kokomo**

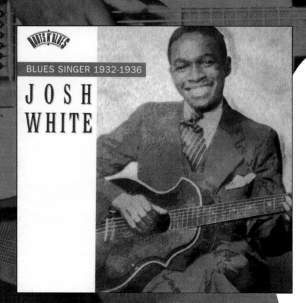

BLUES SINGER 1932-1936
JOSH WHITE

JOSH WHITE

BLUES SINGER

(Columbia Legacy CK 67001)
has some of his earliest work along with sessions with piano that fit neatly into the Leroy Carr/Scrapper Blackwell pattern. (White may actually have recorded with Carr and Blackwell, but nothing from that session is included.) The reissue engineers went a bit too far in removing the surface noise, sometimes distorting the music.

Arnold (1901-1968). It was probably the best-selling guitar blues record of the entire decade, a standard that inspired an "answer" song by Robert Johnson ("Milkcow's Calf Blues") and a Sun Records rockabilly version by Elvis Presley ("Milkcow Blues Boogie") among dozens of other covers. The B-side, "Old Original Kokomo Blues" (based on a Scrapper Blackwell song), directly inspired Robert Johnson's "Sweet Home Chicago" which of course is another of blues' most familiar songs. Arnold never produced anything else of similar significance, though he recorded some 80 further sides for Decca, many of which demonstrate his dextrous slide guitar work (he liked to slide almost the entire length of the guitar neck) and his exciting three-against-two crossrhythms.

Sleepy John Estes (1904-1977) grew up in Brownsville, fifty miles northeast of Memphis; his blues are full of fascinating references to the people and places of his hometown. Together with Brownsville harp player Hammie Nixon he was part of the Memphis jug band scene in the late 1920s. He made some fine records for Victor starting in 1929, but his greatest success was on Decca starting in 1935. All three singles from his first Decca sessions (with Nixon) were hits ("Someday Baby" became a long-running standard) and Estes continued to have regular record releases until World War II.

Sleepy John was a fairly basic guitar player, but his high voice reaches out and grabs you as he sings about a girlfriend's house burning down, his faithful Model T Ford, a night in a hobo jungle, the day he almost drowned in a flood, or the town lawyer who could prove that water runs upstream. Music has never been more intensely personal. (Having used the blues reviewer's most worn-out cliche for the man whose blues most deserves it, we will now retire "intensely personal"!)

He tried a comeback for Sun Records in Memphis in April 1952; the recordings weren't released until after his death. About this time he went blind, and lived in poverty in Brownsville until his "rediscovery" in 1962 led to some fine LPs for the Delmark label.

Most blues recording in the 1930s was done in either New York or Chicago. Every so often, though, Bluebird and Vocalion sent crews with some semi-portable equipment to places like Atlanta, Charlotte,

SLEEPY JOHN ESTES

I AIN'T GONNA BE WORRIED NO MORE
(Yazoo 2004)
A great selection covering his Victor and Decca periods.

THE LEGEND OF SLEEPY JOHN ESTES
(Delmark DD 603)
His fine comeback album.

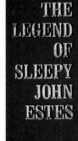

New Orleans, Dallas or San Antonio to record local talent. This included pop, country and ethnic music as well as blues. Lester Melrose was not involved in these endeavors.

In November 1936, Vocalion's crew set up shop in San Antonio. They were there to record several country artists, some Mexican music, and also a young blues singer-guitarist from the Mississippi Delta. The Delta really hadn't been heard from since Charlie Patton died in 1934, and none of its hard-core blues had ever done any business north of Memphis up to that point, but this young man had built up quite a reputation locally and Vocalion decided to give him a shot. His name was Robert Johnson.

◆

Robert Johnson (1911-1938) reigns today as the most celebrated and influential blues performer of the genre's first half century. *Robert Johnson: The Complete Recordings* (Columbia, 1990) is the most successful CD package of pre-WWII recordings ever released, of any type of music.

Johnson took the basic Mississippi Delta blues to a new level of intensity. His guitar technique set the all time standard for the Delta style. Most exceptional of all are his lyrics. He unerringly adopted the very best of the Delta's catalog of floating blues lines, while contributing many apparently original verses that rank among the blues' most profound and poetic creations.

What little we know of his short life has only added to the Robert Johnson legend. Once he took up guitar, he developed his artistry very quickly. Couple that with the Satanic references and general paranoia in "Hell Hound On My Trail," "Crossroads" and other songs, and you can understand the popular belief that Johnson traded his soul to the devil in exchange for his artistry... the myth that inspired the 1986 feature film *Crossroads* among other things.

His 1936 San Antonio sessions produced one fairsized local hit, "Terraplane Blues"...enough to warrant a second group of sessions in Dallas in June 1937. His records were sold mainly in the Delta; there was no real effort to promote them nationally. However, the eminent New York record producer and concert promoter John Hammond, Sr. came across a few of them in the fall of 1938. Amazed, he decided to bring Robert Johnson to New York and have him perform in Carnegie Hall. But it was too late...Johnson had been murdered in August.

A decade later, a new blues boom began in Chicago. At the center of it was Muddy Waters. As a young man in Mississippi, Johnson had been his idol. Muddy performed and recorded several of Johnson's songs in the late 1940s and early 1950s. Johnny Shines, who had known Johnson well, also recorded at that time, and Elmore James turned a Johnson song into his signature piece, "Dust My Broom."

But Johnson himself remained virtually forgotten until 1959. That year, a reverent chapter about him appeared in Samuel Charters' *The Country Blues*, the first decent book to be written on blues as a whole. "Preachin' Blues" appeared on the accompanying LP, the first-ever reissue of a Johnson song.

In 1962 Columbia released 16 songs on an LP called *Robert Johnson: King of the Delta Blues Singers*. You'd be hard-pressed to find a white blues performer over 40 today whose life wasn't profoundly changed by that record. Many of them covered Johnson's songs—Paul Butterfield ("Walkin' Blues"), Eric Clapton ("Crossroads" with Cream), The Rolling Stones ("Love In Vain").

If you've seen that album, you may have noticed there was no photo of Johnson on it—in 1962, no photo of him was known to exist. The album note writer could only find a few scraps of hearsay about his life. It's hard to imagine that someone whose greatness seems so obvious today could have passed into such obscurity...but the fact is that when he was alive, Robert Johnson was no more than a blip on the screen of the music industry. Outside of the Delta (where few people could afford to buy his records) the urban blues of Big Bill, Washboard Sam and the Harlem Hamfats ruled the day. Music like Johnson's was considered outdated stuff for back-country cotton-pickers. Aside from "Terraplane Blues" nothing of his sold very well, not even matching the modest but steady record sales of other rural artists like Sleepy John Estes or Blind Boy Fuller. As a result, his 78s quickly went out of print, and soon became almost impossible to find. Not a one was reissued until 1959. Eventually, their rarity itself helped to build the Robert Johnson legend.

We now know that Robert Johnson was born May 8, 1911 in the southern Mississippi town of Hazlehurst to unmarried parents. He was raised partly in Memphis. His first instrument was harmonica. An older brother gave him his first guitar lessons. In his late teens he lived in the Delta and saw live performances by Charlie Patton and Son House, around the time they made their first records.

House often told interviewers about how young Robert made a pest of himself, trying to pick up the older man's guitar technique without much immediate success. Later, Johnson's records would show that he'd absorbed a whole lot of House's music. Two of his finest pieces, "Preachin' Blues" and "Walkin' Blues," are essentially Son House covers.

At about age 18, Johnson married a woman who died in childbirth. He returned to his hometown of Hazlehurst and soon married again. We now know that he stayed there for a couple of years, and polished his guitar technique with the help of a local musician named Ike Zinnerman, before returning to the Delta.

When Son House first saw him after this absence, not knowing where he had been, he was totally astounded by Robert's sudden metamorphosis into an ace guitarist and charismatic performer.

That was about 1933. From then on, Johnson lived the life of an itinerant entertainer. He visited St. Louis, Chicago, Detroit and New York, but performed most often in the Delta, at parties and "jook joints." In addition to Shines, he played with Robert Lockwood, who later began calling himself "Robert Jr." Lockwood in Johnson's honor. Most often, though, Johnson travelled and performed on his own.

ROBERT JOHNSON

THE COMPLETE RECORDINGS

(Columbia 46222)

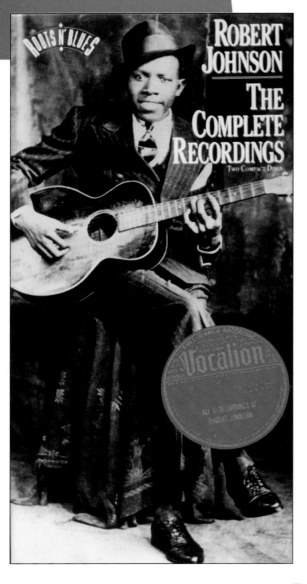

Though he was best known for his blues, he is also known to have sung and played many other kinds of music—pop songs new and old, country songs, and all kinds of dance tunes. Those who were there clearly remember him singing and playing "Yes Sir, That's My Baby," "My Blue Heaven," and "Tumbling Tumbleweeds." It's said that he could learn almost anything after hearing it just once, in person, on the radio or on a record. You can hear the influence of various recording artists in his work: Kokomo Arnold ("Sweet Home Chicago"), Skip James ("32-20 Blues"), Leroy Carr ("Love In Vain") and one he especially admired, Lonnie Johnson ("Drunken Hearted Man").

After his second recording session failed to produce any hits big enough to change the course of his career, Robert was soon back to his ramblings. If he had a home in his last years, it was in Helena, Arkansas, just across the river from Mississippi.

Robert was known to take a drink, and was also what one might today call a womanizer. He was performing at a jook joint near Greenwood, Miss., when the owner became annoyed at Johnson's intense interest in his wife. The next time Robert asked for whiskey, he got the house special, with strychnine added. The King of the Delta Blues Singers died on August 16, 1938, aged 27.

It may be idle to speculate about what he might have accomplished had he lived longer...but what blues fan hasn't done that? One can certainly imagine him going to Chicago after the war and plugging in like Muddy and Johnny Shines and Robert Junior Lockwood did. His onetime idol Lonnie Johnson had a big career surge in the late 1940s with the pop ballad "Tomorrow Night." Robert knew a lot of songs like that. But suppose he'd given that performance at Carnegie Hall...would he have been adopted by New York's folk music revival audience like Leadbelly and Josh White were? Johnson might have known as many "folk songs" as either of them; too bad Vocalion Records wasn't interested in those. Or, like so many others, he just might have sought refuge from his demons by giving up blues to sing for the Lord.

In any case, the records he left behind still provide, 60-plus years later, as exciting and profound a listening experience as blues (or any other music) has to offer.

◆

There was one other Mississippi guitar man who made some noise for Vocalion in the late 1930s—one of his records, to tell the truth, probably sold more 78s than Robert Johnson's entire output combined. The record was "Shake 'Em On Down" and the singer was **Bukka White** (1909-1977). The man's name was actually Booker T. Washington White; he'd made a few sides in 1930 as "Washington White." He wasn't much on reading and writing, and when someone at Vocalion asked him his name in 1937, and he said "Booker," it was written down phonetically, and there you have it.

Born in the northeastern Mississippi hill country near Aberdeen, White spent some time in the Delta hanging around Charlie Patton & Co. before settling in Memphis. A big, burly man, he was a pro ballplayer in the Negro leagues. In 1937 he was arrested for shooting a man; he jumped bail to go to Chicago where he recorded "Shake 'Em On Down" for Lester Melrose. The law caught up with him and sent him to Mississippi's infamous Parchman Farm, where he recorded a few songs for one of Alan Lomax's collecting expeditions.

Bukka was released in 1940, and finally got to go back to Chicago and do a proper followup for Melrose. His 12-song session (with just his guitar and Washboard Sam for backup) produced no commercial hits...but song for song, there's never been a greater blues recording session. "Fixin' To Die" in particular captivated a whole generation of young listeners when it was reissued in 1959; Bob Dylan was among the first to cover it. "Sleepy Man Blues," "Aberdeen Mississippi Blues," "Good Gin Blues," "Strange Place Blues" (about the death of his mother) and two songs about Parchman Farm are just some of the immensely profound songs Bukka laid down that day.

With no sales, there were no more sessions, so Bukka went back to Memphis and became a laborer. During this period he did get acquainted with a young lad named Riley B. King, his first cousin's son; Riley would later become better known as B.B. King. But there wasn't much work in music for Bukka until guitarist/researcher John Fahey and his friend Ed Denson tracked him down in 1963 and signed him to their Takoma label. Sounding as fine as ever, Bukka played many coffeehouses and festivals for the next few years, and made several splendid comeback albums.

Tommy McClennan (1908-1962) from Yazoo City, Miss., had a Delta sound that was harder and harsher than Bukka's, but Lester Melrose liked him enough to record 40 of his blues in Chicago between 1939 and 1942. His big song was the hard-driving "Bottle Up and Go." One of its verses contains the N-word, perhaps the last time it was used by an African-American on a good-selling record until the days of Richard Pryor and rap. It was rare for blues on commercially made records to mention black-white relationships in any context. Other than that McClennan wasn't much of a songwriter; many of his songs were thinly disguised covers of other people's hits. It's often obvious that he was well into a bottle while recording. But you won't often hear more passionate blues, or blues where the passion comes closer to crossing over into rage. A friend of McClennan's, Robert Petway, made some sides in a very similar style about this time, including the first-ever version of the standard "Catfish Blues." McClennan stayed in Chicago for 20 years after his last session for Melrose; for whatever reason, he never could get another

BUKKA WHITE

THE COMPLETE BUKKA WHITE

(Columbia 52782)

TOMMY McCLENNAN

THE BLUEBIRD RECORDINGS

(RCA 67430)

His complete recorded works on two CDs.

John Lee **"Sonny Boy"** **Williamson** was a 23-year-old singer and harmonica player from Jackson, Tennessee, when he cut his first session for Bluebird Records and Lester Melrose in 1937. He started with a bang: the very first song he cut was "Good Morning (Little) School Girl," his best-known original and a standard to this day.

record date. "He really hated white people," recalled 1960s guitar hero Mike Bloomfield, who met McClennan shortly before he died of alcoholism.

Bloomfield also got to know **Big Joe Williams** (a.k.a. Poor Joe Williams, 1903-1982). He wrote a little book called *Me and Big Joe* which has some wonderful anecdotes about this eccentric nine-string guitarist. (It's even more revealing about the young white guitarist's struggle to get inside African-American culture.)

Williams will go down in history as the composer of "Baby, Please Don't Go," a four-line, one-chord song that gets close to the heart of what blues is all about. "Crawlin' King Snake" is another standard from his pen. His pre-WWII recording career never quite took off, despite two fine versions of "Baby, Please Don't Go," but he kept at it through the electric 1950s and became a great favorite of the blues revival in the 1960s. He played concerts and festivals around the world until shortly before his death.

BIG JOE WILLIAMS

COMPLETE RECORDED WORKS IN CHRONOLOGICAL ORDER, Vol. 1

(Document 6003)

Williamson was the most important, in the long run, of all the artists Lester Melrose introduced to the world. His harmonica playing completely revolutionized the role of the instrument, with its agressive attack, loud and hard tone, heavily bent notes, and energetic phrasing. Most modern-day blues harmonica can be traced back to Sonny Boy, at least indirectly. He was also a fine singer, whose natural speech impediment became part of his style and was even imitated by others, years afterward. Like Melrose's other popular artists, he would crank out enough recordings to have a new single every month, even when he didn't have enough good original songs to fill them all (he recorded 18 songs on July 21, 1939, for instance) but his musicianship makes every one a treat.

As time went on Melrose added pianos and rhythm sections to the mix (at least there weren't any clarinets) and Sonny Boy still took charge just like he always had. When he resumed recording for Melrose after World War II, he sounded even better than before (he was the only one of Melrose's many artists you could say that about). Sonny Boy Williamson might still be blowing the blues today if he hadn't been waylaid by a robber who stabbed him to death with an icepick in front of his Chicago home. Sonny Boy was 34.

Even before that, another fine singer/harmonica man named Aleck "Rice" Miller decided to bill himself as Sonny Boy Williamson, thereby causing endless confusion which has only been partly resolved by historians' general agreement that the man we've just discussed shall be known as Sonny Boy Williamson #1, and Miller as Sonny Boy Williamson #2. Remember that when we meet Number Two in the next chapter!

Another Melrose discovery, Doctor Clayton, recorded "Pearl Harbor Blues" in March 1942, heralding the war that would shake up the blues world as it did everything else in American life. Bluesmen who

SONNY BOY WILLIAMSON

THE BLUEBIRD RECORDINGS 1937-1938

(RCA 66723)

THE BLUEBIRD RECORDINGS 1938

(RCA 66796)

didn't get drafted kept on playing parties, jook joints and beer taverns as they always had…but for two years hardly a note was recorded. A shortage of shellac, the raw material for 78 rpm records, was bad enough; the musician's union compounded things by calling a nationwide strike against the record industry.

After the war, blues would be changed even more profoundly by another great event: the massive migration of African-Americans from the rural South to the urban North, East and West. The music of the new migrants would soon drive blues into its next era of greatness.

The Shouters

It was sometimes hard to tell where blues stopped and jazz began in the 1940s. Count Basie's big band blues of the 1930s (with vocalist Jimmy Rushing) was widely emulated by singers and instrumentalists even after the big bands gave way to small combos. Many singers with a jazz background flourished on the late 1940s blues scene, and a few were able to continue their careers with great success even after the heyday of this kind of blues had passed. The most revered has to be **Big Joe Turner** (1911-1985). He was born and raised in Kansas City, Basie's home base and a hotbed

of jazz in the 1920s and '30s. Like Rushing, he was a "shouter" who phrased his lines more like a jazz instrumental soloist than like a traditional blues singer…and like Rushing, he had the decibels to soar above a big band.

In the 1930s, Turner often sang with local boogie-woogie pianist Pete Johnson. When Johnson became a national celebrity during the boogie-woogie craze (see p. 76), Turner often joined him in concert and on records. Through the 1940s Big Joe had steady nightclub work and recorded frequently, but his best years

were still to come. In 1951 he signed with Atlantic Records…and the next thing you knew, he was a 43-year-old, 300-pound rock 'n' roll star. A series of smartly produced singles including "Chains Of Love," "Honey Hush," "Shake, Rattle and Roll" and "Corrine Corrina" made him one of the giants of 1950s R&B while hardly changing a lick of his Swing Era singing style. When the R&B hits eventually stopped coming, he had no trouble easing back into the jazz world. He was a frequent honored guest at jazz and blues festivals alike, still ringing the rafters well into his 70s, even after he could no longer stand up on stage.

In the late 1940s, before Big Joe got his second wind, the most popular "shouter" was **Wynonie Harris** (1915-1969) from Omaha. In 1944 he hooked up with Lucky Millinder's big band and sang on Millinder's crossover novelty hit "Who Threw the Whiskey In the Well" (#7 on the pop charts in 1945). His solo career took off soon thereafter, topped by "Good Rockin' Tonight" (a 1948 disc that sounds very much indeed like rock 'n' roll, half a decade early), "All She Wants To Do Is Rock" and "Good Morning Judge." Unlike Big Joe he was a slim, good lookin' dude with a stage show that was athletic to the point of lewdness. Elvis Presley covered "Good Rockin'" and, the story goes, some of Wynonie's moves as well. But again unlike Big Joe, when rock 'n' roll came in Wynonie was unable to capitalize, and his career fell by the wayside in the 1950s. He was a hard drinker, notoriously unreliable, and apparently paid the price.

"Good Rockin' Tonight" was actually written and originally recorded by another ace shouter, New Orleans' **Roy Brown** (1925-1981). Wynonie beat him out on that one, but Brown had a long string of hits in the late 1940s and early 1950s including "'Long About Midnight," "Boogie At Midnight," "Hard Luck Blues" and the raunchy "Butcher Pete." Roy was really at his best on slow blues, where he could get the most out of his high, clear, gorgeous voice. He probably sounded a bit too "legit" for the rock 'n' roll crowd, which shunned his attempts to rock out in 1956. The blues revival crowd was just beginning to get hip to him when he died at age 55.

BIG, BAD AND BLUE: THE BIG JOE TURNER ANTHOLOGY

(Rhino 71550)
Three CDs spanning his entire career.

Bull Moose Jackson (Benjamin Jackson, 1919-1989; he preferred to be called simply "Moose") was a big band shouter who became best known in 1947-48 for his blues ballads ("I Love You, Yes I Do" and "I Can't Go On Without You"). Four years later, he recorded the delightfully suggestive "Big Ten-Inch *(pause)* Record*," covered by Aerosmith on *Toys in the Attic*. In the 1980s, a Pittsburgh retro-rock band called The Flashcats made it their mission to bring Moose back from oblivion; he recorded a fine live album with them.

Two notable shouters who split the difference between blues and jazz: **Joe Williams** (1918-1999) sang with the Count Basie band of the 1950s and had a surprise hit with "Every Day (I Have the Blues)" in 1956. It was a cover of B.B. King's cover of Lowell Fulson's cover of a Memphis Slim song originally called "Nobody Loves Me," but it was a knockout performance. **Jimmy Witherspoon** (1923-1997) had an R&B #1 in 1949 with "Ain't Nobody's Business," originally recorded by Bessie Smith in 1922 and followed that with a version of Leroy Carr's "In The Evening When The Sun Goes Down." "Spoon" was a keen student of the history of both jazz and blues, and a very articulate man, who soldiered on despite an episode of throat cancer in the early 1980s. His story is well told in Chip Deffaa's book *Blue Rhythms*.

BLOODSHOT EYES: THE BEST OF WYNONIE HARRIS

(Rhino R2-71544)
All the hits from the glory days.

BULL MOOSE JACKSON, THAT'S ME

(Charly [UK] 274)

GOOD ROCKING TONIGHT: THE BEST OF ROY BROWN

(Rhino R2-71545)
All the good ones, fast and slow. Jackie Wilson learned a lot from Roy.

* Most 78 rpm records were ten inches in diameter.

Jimmie Rodgers
America's Blue Yodeler
Victor Recording Star

Can Blue Men Sing the Whites?

—Satiric song by the Bonzo Dog Doo-dah Band, 1968

"Can white men sing the blues?" That question was often asked in the oh-so-serious 1960s, a decade in which a number of talented young Caucasian singers began singing blues, first with acoustic guitars and then electrically. It was argued that because only blacks had experienced the conditions that gave birth to blues, only blacks were entitled to perform blues. Many writers of that time defined blues on strictly racial lines.

That question hasn't seemed to bother many people at any other period of blues history. Certainly not today, with blues being the most thoroughly integrated music genre in the Western world. And definitely not in the 1920s, when white country singers and white pop singers too sang blues, or at least an exciting imitation of blues, with enthusiasm and sometimes with skill.

Though blues is quintessentially African-American music, Caucasians have been part of its orbit for a long, long time. Before the Civil War, slaves regularly sang and played for their masters, and the end of slavery did not by any means end white people's enjoyment of those black singers and musicians.

Most blues artists who grew up in the early 20th century performed for white listeners at least now and then. Some, like the Mississippi Sheiks, played for more white audiences than black ones. Though they typically learned pop songs and country tunes for these occasions, they also played blues…which was often much appreciated and eventually imitated by any neophyte white guitar pickers and singers who happened to be in the audience.

In 1927, a young white Mississippi-born singer named **Jimmie Rodgers** (1897-1933) began his recording career, which would soon make him country music's first superstar. His second release, and first hit, was "Blue Yodel"—a simple 12-bar blues, with amusing, imaginative

VICTOR

His Master's Voice

Orthophonic Recording

For best results use Victor Needles

23696-A

BLUE YODEL No. 10
(Ground Hog Rootin' In My Back Yard)
(J. Rodgers)
Jimmie Rodgers
Singing with guitar

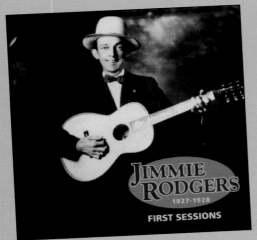

lyrics, and a four-bar yodel after each stanza. Fully one-fourth of the songs he recorded before his death (from tuberculosis at age 35) were in blues form.

Rodgers always said he heard the blues sung by black men he worked with on the railroads. We also know that he was an avid record collector. Unfortunately no one ever wrote down the contents of his collection, but it's reasonable to assume that it included Bessie Smith or other vaudeville blues artists, and quite possibly a disc or two by Blind Lemon, Lonnie Johnson or Barbecue Bob. Though he didn't cover any specific blues records by black artists, verses from black tradition are scattered through his otherwise original Blue Yodels.

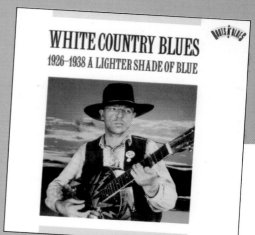

Rodgers wasn't the first country singer to record blues—West Virginia's Frank Hutchison had cut some fine blues in 1926—but due to his great nationwide success, Rodgers was highly influential. One of his first disciples was the young Gene Autry, who recorded so many blues songs early in his career that an entire CD of them was released recently. The Carlisle Brothers, Cliff and Bill, had many country blues hits, together and singly; Cliff was a swell slide guitar player.

In the mid-1930s a new brand of dance music swept the South and ultimately the nation. Played by bands that combined country fiddles with a modern swing beat (and sometimes a swing band's horn section), this music came to be known as "western swing." Among the top bands were Milton Brown (until his death in 1935), the Light Crust Doughboys and Bob Wills and his Texas Playboys, ultimately the most famous. All of them played and recorded blues songs, which they learned primarily from "race records."

Wills' band remained popular after World War II, when several major postwar country singers also added their voices to the blues canon—particularly

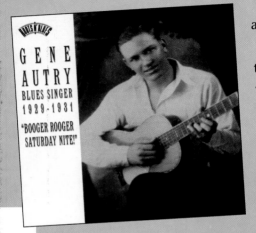

Hank Williams Sr., who credited a black street singer named Tee-Tot with teaching him some of his first guitar chords, and Lefty Frizzell, who recorded an album of Jimmie Rodgers favorites including several blues.

And then along came rockabilly. As the early 1950s R&B craze spread, country singers began covering R&B hits, especially the bluesier ones. One of rock 'n' roll pioneer Bill Haley's first national hits was a cover of Big Joe Turner's "Shake, Rattle and Roll"—not a very convincing performance as far as blues feeling goes, but helping to spread the word nonetheless. Meanwhile, in Memphis, local record entrepreneur Sam Phillips, who had dreamed for years of finding a young, good-looking white singer who could put across some of the blues feeling he heard from Howlin' Wolf, Doctor Ross and other black bluesmen he'd recorded, found the answer to his prayers when young Elvis Presley walked through his studio door.

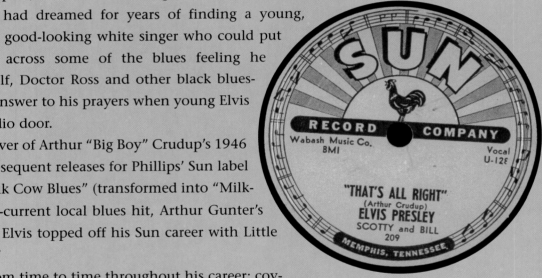

Presley's first single was a cover of Arthur "Big Boy" Crudup's 1946 blues hit "That's All Right." Subsequent releases for Phillips' Sun label included Kokomo Arnold's "Milk Cow Blues" (transformed into "Milk-cow Blues Boogie") and a then-current local blues hit, Arthur Gunter's "Baby Let's Play House" before Elvis topped off his Sun career with Little Junior Parker's "Mystery Train."

Presley returned to blues from time to time throughout his career; covers of Chuck Willis' "Feel So Bad" and Lowell Fulson's "Reconsider Baby" are standouts. While these are more a case of Elvis singing the blues in his own style than any attempt to remake himself as an "authentic" bluesman, he was better at it than most of his immediate white contemporaries.

After 1960, country music went in another direction that rarely touched on blues. You couldn't keep the Caucasian race away from that stuff for long, though! In the early 1960s, a new generation of white singers raised the blues flag high, in both Britain and the U.S.A. See "The Revival Blues."

What the Heck Is a Tympany Anyway?

If any one song could stand for the spirit of America as we tried to get World War II behind us and enjoy some prosperity, it was "Choo Choo Ch'Boogie" by **Louis Jordan** (1908-1975) and his Tympany Five.

Louis formed the Tympany Five in 1938 after a couple of years of playing alto sax and singing in Chick Webb's big band. He was promptly signed to Decca Records, which released many of his records in what they called a "Sepia Series," a presumed allusion to his audience's interracial nature. His records started hitting big just as war was breaking out. Decca Records settled with the musicians' union in mid-1943, a year before the other majors labels did, largely so they could record Jordan again. For the next few years he turned out one #1 hit after another—"Caldonia," "G. I. Jive," "Buzz Me," "Stone Cold Dead In the Market" (with Ella Fitzgerald), "Ain't Nobody Here But Us Chickens," " "Saturday Night Fish Fry." He was the big exception to the majors' otherwise near-total collapse in the black music field.

Jordan played a stripped-down, sped-up version of big band blues like Count Basie's. People called it "jump blues." It featured Jordan's alto sax, trumpet, piano and a rhythm section. A great showman, he specialized in humorous material (mostly written by others) which he delivered with zing and gusto and excellent diction. He appeared in several Hollywood features as well as many short films. Jordan was an all-around entertainer rather than a hard-core bluesman, but his popularity opened a lot of doors for urban blues, and those uptempo shuffle-rhythm songs he did were contagious and widely imitated.

In the mid-1990s a musical revue based on Jordan's repertoire, *Five Guys Named Moe*, created a sensation and a lot of interest in the original recordings. (By the way, "tympany" means "bombast," and has nothing to do with "tympani" [kettledrums]).

THE BEST OF LOUIS JORDAN
(MCA MCAD 4079)

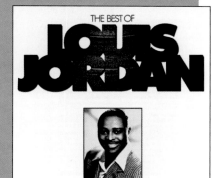

PART THREE

BLUES ON THE MOVE

On October 2, 1944, on a cotton plantation just outside Clarksdale, Mississippi, an event was held that would change millions of lives forever. It was an event comparable in its importance to African-American history to the World War that was just then reaching its climax in Europe and the Pacific.

That event was the first public demonstration of the first practical cotton-picking machine.

Cotton picking by hand is incredibly tedious and back-breaking labor, but before that October day there was simply no other way to harvest the fine cotton fiber that Americans loved to wear. The whole Southern share-cropping system with all its attendant miseries was based on the need for large numbers of bodies willing to do this work, and the scarcity of alternative sources of income for Southern rural blacks.

Plantation owners were overjoyed with the new machinery. No longer did they have to share their crops with their laborers. No longer did they have to provide housing, education and other services for them. They bought those cotton-pickers as fast as the factories could make them.

As for the laborers…they were out of a job, and there weren't many other jobs to be had for blacks in places like the Delta. Only a fortunate bit of timing averted social catastrophe.

World War II soon ended, followed by the greatest boom times ever for American manufacturing. Everyone wanted new cars, refrigerators, radios — all the things that had been unavailable during the war. American factories, still heavily dependent on manual labor in the 1940s and little affected by foreign competition, needed all the workers they could get. The word quickly spread to the rural South, and soon black families by the hundreds of thousands were headed to the cities, joining those who had migrated earlier to work in defense plants.

People from certain rural areas tended to go to certain urban areas…people from the Southeast to the Northeast, people from Texas and Oklahoma to California, and people from the Mississippi Delta, northern Louisiana and Arkansas to Chicago and Detroit. There were of course many exceptions to those trends, but the postwar blues of California has very close ties to Texas, and that of Chicago even stronger ties to the Delta.

Another trend that began right around the time that mechanical cotton-picker was demonstrated in

October 1944 may not have affected the lives of millions of people, but it had a lot to do with the evolution of postwar blues.

Background: In July 1942 the musicians' union called a strike against the American record industry. It was a very effective strike; virtually no musical instruments were heard on any American records for over a year, and some of the biggest labels did not settle with the union until late 1944. Meanwhile, shellac, the chief raw material for records, became impossible to obtain from India due to the war in the Pacific. So the record industry all but shut down.

When blues recording resumed as the war was ending, the major labels basically picked up where they'd left off…which meant lots more Lester Melrose sessions. Unfortunately, the man seemed to lose a lot of his touch during his long vacation. Worse, he all but ignored the flood of new talent that appeared at the end of the war, preferring to try and crank more hits out of Big Bill and Washboard Sam. (He did record Muddy Waters, but the results were not released.) RCA Victor and Columbia relied on him until 1953, but with a few exceptions the quality and commercial success of his products just weren't what they'd been.

Nature abhors a vacuum, of course, and so does American industry. In 1944, a new UCLA business school graduate named Art Rupe took a careful survey of the business climate of Los Angeles, and found that one of the great opportunities was in making records of the new styles of African-American music that were not being recorded by the major record labels. After getting a little experience with existing companies, he started what became Specialty Records, choosing that name because black music was to be his specialty. At the same time, other entrepreneurs in L.A. and other cities were making the same move. By the time the majors knew what had hit them it was far too late. For the next 20 years the story of recorded blues was essentially the story of Specialty Records, and King Records, and Chess Records, and Atlantic, Aladdin, Imperial, Exclusive, Apollo, Savoy, Herald, Vee-Jay, Sensation, Gold Star, Cobra, Chance, Parrot, United, States and hundreds more independent labels, with only occasional contributions from the erstwhile giants of the industry.

More record companies meant more blues records by more blues singers.

More singers meant a greater variety of styles, which flourished simultaneously and constantly influenced each other.

In our next chapter we'll look at how the urban blues of the late 1930s branched out into a variety of wonderful things in the 1940s, especially on the West Coast. Afterward we'll check out the postwar blues renaissance in Chicago, and some new developments in the South.

Chapter **6**
West Coast Jump

If there was one record that made it clear that the new independent record labels were on to something that had eluded the majors, it was "The Honeydripper" by **Joe Liggins** (1915-1987) on the Exclusive label of Los Angeles. Released in 1945, this ultra-hip dance tune featuring tenor sax and piano was by far the biggest "race" record of the year. Bluesman Roosevelt Sykes, who had been calling himself "The Honey Dripper" for years, was rushed into the studio by Lester Melrose to record a cover proclaiming himself "The Original Honeydripper"—but Sykes just didn't have that hip new Honeydripper beat. Neither did Jimmie Lunceford's big band, which covered the tune for Decca. The Liggins version beat them both by miles.*

---

* This despite the fact that Exclusive charged $1.05 a copy for its single, while one could pick up Lunceford's version for 50¢ and Sykes' for 35¢! The latter two were on major labels that had practically cornered the wartime U.S. supply of shellac. Labels like Exclusive had to rely on recycled shellac, made from old 78s which were bought from whoever would sell them, and ground up into powder. Much as one might love the hip R&B hits of the mid-1940s, one winces at the thought of all the pre-war treasures that were sacrificed to make them!

"The Honeydripper" wasn't strictly a blues, but Liggins demonstrated his suave urban blues singing and piano playing on many other records, especially his 1951 hit "Pink Champagne" for Specialty. He could still be heard playing his original 1940s jump blues around L.A. clear into the 1980s. (Joe's younger brother Jimmy Liggins went from being Joe's chauffeur to a fairly successful recording artist in his own right, also on Specialty. His hits included a snappy "Cadillac Boogie" and a song that got right to the point— "Drunk").

The Liggins brothers were just two stars in a whole new galaxy of West Coast urban bluesmen. Before the war, record companies just hadn't bothered to look for blues on the West Coast. The new labels that opened up as the war was ending found plenty, nourished by the thousands of African-Americans arriving every year from Texas and Oklahoma. Specialty Records landed one of the biggest stars in town, **Roy Milton** (1907-1983), who like the Liggins brothers hailed from Oklahoma. Milton and his

JOE LIGGINS

AND THE HONEYDRIPPERS

(Specialty SPCD 7006)
His Specialty hits plus an acceptable note-for-note remake of "The Honeydripper."

Solid Senders had been playing a mixture of urban blues and swinging dance music around L.A. since the mid-1930s, featuring Roy's vocals and drumming and Camille Howard on piano.

Milton's first and biggest hit, "R.M. Blues" (1945), is archetypical 1940s urban blues. The restrained but eloquent vocal and prominent piano recall prewar Lester Melrose sessions, but on "R.M. Blues" the rhythmic feel is hipper, more danceable...it almost bumps and grinds! And dig those rocking piano triplets and those hypnotic horn riffs! Ol' Lester never did catch on to stuff like that. Rock 'n' roll borrowed a lot from urban blues like this.

Along with blues, fast and slow, Milton sang what were called "blues ballads"—songs with Tin Pan Alley's 32-bar harmonic structure rather than the 12-bar blues chorus, but sung and played with the same feeling as urban blues. There'd been a few of these before the war—"Romance In the Dark" by Lil Green with Big Bill Broonzy for example—but the form really came into its own in the mid-1940s. One of the

first-ever hit records by a black artist on an independent label was a blues ballad, "I Wonder" sung by Private **Cecil Gant** (1913-1951) in a voice faintly reminiscent of Leroy Carr's, on the Gilt-Edge label of Los Angeles. It was just a wisp of a song, with the simplest of rhymes and absolutely none of the clever turns of phrase beloved by the songsmiths,

ROY MILTON

AND HIS SOLID SENDERS

(Specialty SPCD 7004)

but it perfectly nailed the mood of a couple of million soldiers and their far-away loved ones in 1944. When Gilt-Edge couldn't get enough shellac to fill the demand, they pressed it on cardboard, complete with a smiling photo of Pvt. Gant. Cecil was pretty much a one-hit wonder (he drank himself to death at 37) but he left his mark: practically every late 1940s urban bluesman had some blues ballads in his repertoire. (Similarly simple 32-bar ballads later became *de riguer* for "doo-wop" vocal groups.)

No one sings blues ballads better than **Charles Brown** (1922-1999), another Texas transplant who hit it big in L.A. Charles Brown is unique among bluesmen for a lot of reasons. He was raised in a middle-class home, studying classical piano. He got a college degree in chemistry. He became a fan of jazz and pop music first; jazz pianist Art Tatum and pop singer Helen O'Connell remain his favorites. Blues came later. To make a long story short, he was working in a shipyard in Los Angeles when he entered a talent show and won first prize, playing a boogie-woogie followed by a classical piece. That led to his joining a trio led by Johnny Moore, brother of Nat King Cole's guitarist Oscar Moore. They wanted someone to play piano and sing ballads kinda like Nat; Charles was their man.

Johnny Moore's Three Blazers played for white audiences in Beverly Hills. They only played one blues song per show...but that song, Charles' "Drifting Blues," got the group a deal with Philo Records. Philo, soon renamed Aladdin, was another one of those Los Angeles start-up labels that quickly did very well, with major help from "Drifting Blues." The Blazers followed that up with hit after hit, alternating 12-bar blues with ballads. After Charles went solo in 1949, "Trouble Blues," "Black Night" and the perennial "Merry Christmas Baby" were among his many best-sellers.

There'd never been a blues singer or a blues pianist like Charles Brown. He caressed the keys instead of pounding them. He didn't shout; he crooned. After all, he played cocktail lounges and theatres, not jook joints or barrelhouses. Historians call his music "cocktail blues" (ironic in a way, because Charles didn't touch a drop). It appealed instantly to upwardly mobile postwar African-Americans who shunned most blues because it reminded them of rural squalor, but still felt a little emotional tug from the music.

The latterday Blues Revival audience didn't take to Brown right away, being used to rougher stuff—but

they grew towards each other. For one thing, Brown subtly put just a bit more punch into his music in the 1980s and 1990s. A tour with Bonnie Raitt in 1990 was a turning point, along with Brown's recent albums, quite possibly the best of his long career.

Brown and Dixon were part of a parade of singer-pianists from Texas who hit big in California in the 1940s. **Ivory Joe Hunter** (1914-1974) was another blues ballad specialist, and a fine songwriter. His two best-remembered songs are both 12-bar blues, but with pretty, major-key melodies reflecting the pop influence: "I Almost Lost My Mind" (1950; a 1956 Pat Boone cover was

CHARLES BROWN

ALL MY LIFE

(Bullseye Blues BB 9501)
Possibly the most youthful 70-year-old bluesman ever recorded.

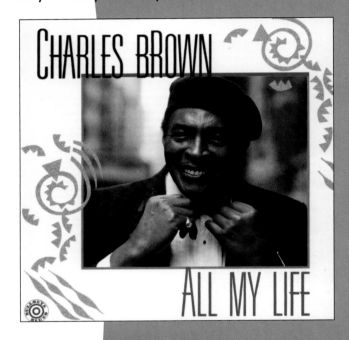

DRIFTIN' BLUES: THE BEST OF CHARLES BROWN

(EMI CDP 97989-2)
The title song and other gems from the 1940s and 1950s.

BOOK: BLUE RHYTHMS: SIX LIVES IN RHYTHM AND BLUES by Chip Deffaa (1996, University of Illinois Press)

Read more about Charles Brown in *Blues Rhythms*. The book also profiles Floyd Dixon, the Texan who replaced Brown in Johnny Moore's Three Blazers, and jazz-blues shouter Jimmy Witherspoon, along with Ruth Brown, LaVern Baker and Little Jimmy Scott.

a huge pop hit and Boone's best blues effort) and "Since I Met You Baby" (1956). **Amos Milburn** (1927-1980) slammed onto the charts in 1950 with the fast and rowdy "Chicken Shack Boogie" and made it a one-two punch with the beautiful blues ballad "Bewildered." Modern blues fans probably know Amos best for his booze blues—"Bad, Bad Whiskey," "One Scotch, One Bourbon, One Beer" (later a hit for George Thorogood), "Thinking and Drinking," "Good, Good Whiskey" and for good measure "Vicious, Vicious Vodka."

Percy Mayfield (1920-1984) was perhaps the finest blues ballad singer of them all, and "Please Send Me Someone To Love" the deepest song ever written in that genre. "The River's Invitation" is another masterpiece. An auto accident in 1952 derailed Percy's career and left him permanently disfigured, but in the late 1950s and early 1960s he recorded for Ray Charles'

THE BEST OF AMOS MILBURN

(EMI 27229)
A good single-disc compilation. A 3-CD set with the same material plus a lot more is available on Capitol.

Tangerine label and also wrote some hits for Ray including "Hit The Road, Jack" which went to Number One. His blues festival appearances won him many new fans just before his death.

◆

The years from 1945 to 1955 could be called "the era of the saxophone." There was quite a cult of "honkers" in those days…tenor sax players whose solos built to an ecstatic frenzy, often climaxing with a minute or two of the same note over and over. It was something to be seen, preferably live, as the soloists writhed on the floor like Holy Rollers, or climbed atop the bar, or the audience. Illinois Jacquet usually gets credit for starting this brand of R&B while playing with Lionel Hampton's band; other sax gods included Hal Singer, Joe Houston, Big Jay McNeely and Red Prysock.

That music may not have been blues in the purest sense…but during that time it seemed there was a tenor sax solo on practically every urban blues record (and, of course, on many examples of what came to be called rock 'n' roll). However, there were a few holdouts for urban blues guitar as a lead instrument. One of those singer-guitarists is now recognized as *the* most influential urban bluesman of the early postwar period.

Aaron Thibeaux **"T-Bone" Walker** (1910-1975) had a career that spanned many periods. He got some of his first guitar lessons from Blind Lemon Jefferson,

PERCY MAYFIELD

POET OF THE BLUES

(Specialty CD 7001)
The original "Please Send Me Someone To Love," "River's Invitation" and much more.

PERCY MAYFIELD LIVE

(Winner 445)
A superb live album from the early 1980s, produced by ex-Butterfield Blues Band keyboardist and radio host Mark Naftalin, who made Mayfield's final comeback possible.

as one of the young lads who would lead Blind Lemon around the streets of Dallas and collect contributions for him. T-Bone learned better than most. At age 19 he was already good enough to get a record released on Columbia...but the real T-Bone Walker story starts half a decade later, after he emigrated (like so many Texans after him) to Los Angeles.

Sometime around 1935 he got a chance to play one of the very first electric guitars ever made. It was a match made in blues heaven. The electric guitar was T-Bone's axe from that day forward. Alas, nobody recorded him in the 1930s. Though all the major labels had studios in Hollywood, no one there seemed to care about the blues scene that was percolating just a few miles away on South Central Avenue.

T-BONE WALKER

BOOK: STORMY MONDAY: THE T-BONE WALKER STORY by Helen Oakley Dance (1987, Louisiana State University Press—reprinted by Da Capo Books, N.Y.)
A warm reminiscence, mostly told in the words of T-Bone, his relatives and friends.

BLUES MASTERS: THE VERY BEST OF T-BONE WALKER
(Rhino R2 79894)

T-Bone probably doesn't play the Hawaiian-style electric guitar on the vocal blues he finally got to record in 1940 in New York with Les Hite's big band. Regardless, "T-Bone Blues" got him enough nationwide attention to go out on his own. And what a show he put on...he was as famous for doing the splits and playing the guitar behind his back as for the fine urban blues he sang and played. Through the decade he packed 'em in at the best African-American nightclubs in the land, and had 'em screaming for more.

His records may be a bit sedate by comparison—but when his recording career resumed after the war the hits came fast and furiously, mostly on Black & White Records, another of those new West Coast independents. In 1947 he first recorded the song that crowned his career, "Call It Stormy Monday." You'd be hard pressed to find a bluesman since who hasn't sung that number. Another 1947 hit was the guitar showpiece "T-Bone Shuffle."

T-Bone's singing is prototypical urban blues—restrained, not showy, but emotional in a subtle way. His guitar reflects a lot of the jazz he heard while he was growing up and the jazz he played down on Central Avenue while waiting for his big break. Whereas the prewar blues lead guitarists like Scrapper Blackwell and Tampa Red always stuck close to the beat, T-Bone's solos are full of little rhythmic excursions. Even at a slow tempo, he'll ease into a little syncopated pattern that makes the music really jump for a line or two, then back into a mellow groove. There's a lot of jazz in T-Bone's harmonies as well: those 12-bar choruses aren't just three chords any more. Though that I-IV-V structure is still recognizable, he'll throw in a lot of extra changes, a lot of augmented and diminished chords and such, to perk things up. Don't expect a lot of those pyrotechnics that audiences have grown used to today when you hear T-Bone. His playing isn't flashy—it's tasty.

The big record hits stopped coming after 1950, but T-Bone's live act kept the crowds coming for many years afterward. A brilliant 1959 LP for Atlantic, *T-Bone Blues*, helped introduce him to Europe where he had a lot of success in the 1960s. By this time, though, a persistent stomach ulcer and alcoholism were taking their toll.

T-Bone didn't live to see the rush of enthusiasm for blues that began at the end of the 1970s...but he can take credit, at least indirectly, for a whole lot of that. The man who set off that blues explosion was B.B. King, and here's what B.B. had to say about T-Bone:

I loved how Lonnie [Johnson] and Blind Lemon and many others played guitar. I was—and still am—a student of the instrument. I was fascinated by the sound. I liked most everything I heard. But when I heard Aaron "T-Bone" Walker, I flat-out lost my mind. Thought Jesus Himself had returned to earth playing electric guitar. T-Bone's blues filled my insides with joy and good feeling. I became his disciple. And remain so today. My greatest musical debt is to T-Bone. He showed me the way. His sound cut me like a sword. His sound was so different than anything I'd heard before. Musically, he was everything I wanted to be, a modern bluesman whose blues were as blue as the bluest country blues with attitude as slick as those big cities I yearned to see." (*Blues All Around Me: The Autobiography of B.B. King*, by B.B. King with David Ritz, 1996, Avon Books, New York, p. 78.)

Lowell Fulson (1921-1999) was another West Coast guitar star of the 1940s, based in Oakland. (His last name is often spelled "Fulsom" on labels.) Unlike T-Bone's, his guitar playing owes more to country blues than to jazz. Indeed, his earliest records are almost pure rural blues, but he became best known for his music in a more urban groove, often with pianist Lloyd Glenn. After a hit version of Memphis Slim's "Everyday I Have The Blues" in 1950, he made #1 on the R&B charts with his original "Blue Shadows." "Reconsider Baby" was big in 1954, and he had another run of hits in the mid-1960s with "Black Nights" and the funky novelty blues "Tramp." Fulson always sang with a little more of what came to be called "soul" than most urban bluesmen, a reflection of the gospel music he heard as a boy in Oklahoma.

LOWELL FULSON

TRAMP & SOUL

(Flair-Virgin 86300)
His sixties hits and more.

Before we leave the West Coast urban blues, let us salute a man who is a category unto himself. **Ray Charles** (1930-) has seemingly done everything that there is to do in music...but he had to start with one thing. At age 18, he moved from Florida to Seattle—and set out to be the Charles Brown of Seattle, with a taste of Nat King Cole on the side. It worked—he had a #2 R&B hit with his very first record release, "Confession Blues" (the first R&B hit ever recorded in Seattle, for sure). As time passed, he started putting a little more soul into that cocktail blues, then a whole lot more. Atlantic Records encouraged this after signing him in 1953, and he soon left behind all signs of urban blues' time-honored restraint and let it all hang out with vocals as sanctified as any gospel singer's. It was soon discovered that Ray could slay people with just about anything he tried, from hard-core jazz to crooning. Most of his career is outside the scope of this book...but those who are tuned in to blues will still hear at least a bit of it in everything Ray Charles does.

RAY CHARLES

THE BIRTH OF A LEGEND

(Ebony CD 8001/2)
His complete pre-Atlantic recordings on 2 CDs. Note: at presstime Rhino is preparing an extensive program of Ray Charles CD reissues.

THE BIRTH OF SOUL: THE COMPLETE ATLANTIC RHYTHM & BLUES RECORDINGS (1952–1959)

(Rhino 2-82310, 3 CD's)

SONNY BOY WILLIAMSON #2:

The Imposter Who Turned Out to Be the Real Thing

It was a little like some small-time entertainer today taking the name Bruce Springsteen or Garth Brooks. Of course, we weren't blessed with today's modern media in 1941, which is when an itinerant singer and harmonica player stepped up to a radio microphone in Helena, Arkansas, and announced that he was **Sonny Boy Williamson**.

At that moment, John Lee "Sonny Boy" Williamson was the most famous blues harmonica man in African America, with many best-selling Bluebird records to his credit. But that Sonny Boy had long since moved to Chicago, and hadn't been seen around Helena in years. Blues singers were rarely seen in print, and television was still on the drawing board, so who'd know the difference? Besides, our new radio star would be playing songs he'd learned off those Bluebird records, along with some of his own.

John Lee Williamson didn't even bother to seek an injunction against the "bogus" Sonny Boy until 1947; he was murdered before any legal action could be consummated. Our radio star then had the name to himself…and he eventually made that name more famous than John Lee ever had, and left a larger footprint upon blues history as well.

The radio man (whom historians call Sonny Boy Williamson #2) was actually older, and had been singing and playing blues longer, than Sonny Boy Williamson #1 (John Lee, that is) had. How much older he was, we don't know for sure. The years 1894, 1897, 1899, 1901, 1908, 1909 and 1910 have all been proclaimed as the date of his birth near Glendora, Miss.; the latest date seems the best bet. His real name was probably Aleck Miller; he was nicknamed "Rice" as a child. As long as he lived, he stonewalled all questions about his past…but by the early 1930s he was a

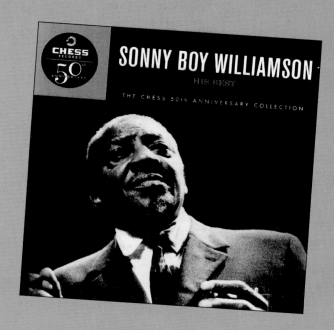

good enough performer so that people remembered him, good enough to earn a few dollars for a bottle and a crap game. "Little Boy Blue" was what they usually called him. He played and travelled a time or two with Robert Johnson, and struck up a more lasting partnership with Johnson's stepson Robert "Junior" Lockwood.

By 1941, when a Helena businessman opened up a new radio station and was looking for programming that appealed to local African-Americans, Little Boy Blue was one of the better known bluesmen in the area. As "Sonny Boy Williamson," singing the praises of King Biscuit Flour on KFFA every weekday at noon and promoting his live gigs, he became the hottest act in town. His fame soon spread well beyond the range of the station's transmitter. A teenaged Riley B. King was just one of many future bluesmen who got the message.

Radio stardom did not change Sonny Boy's ramblin' lifestyle. He frequently left Helena for some other small-town station down the road, but was welcomed back to KFFA when he returned. No one was able to get him into a recording studio until the tiny Trumpet label of Jackson, Miss., pulled it off in January 1951. A dozen Sonny Boy 78s resulted, some of which sold quite well across the South, attracting the interest of Chess Records in Chicago which signed him for its Checker label.

SONNY BOY WILLIAMSON: HIS BEST

(MCA Chess 9377)
"Don't Start Me Talkin'," "Help Me" and the rest of the Chess classics.

Checker's first Sonny Boy release, "Don't Start Me Talkin'," (with Muddy Waters and Jimmy Rogers on guitar) was a hit, and Checker released frequent Sonny Boy singles for the next decade. On many of these he was reunited with Robert "Junior" Lockwood, a regular Chess backup guitarist in the last half

SONNY BOY WILLIAMSON: KING BISCUIT TIME

(Arhoolie 310)
This CD neatly bookends the Chess material, with his early Trumpet sides plus that last King Biscuit Time show in 1965.

of the 1950s. As with Muddy and Wolf, the music he made may have been born in the 1930s, but when conditions were right it meshed perfectly with the electric Chicago sound. Conditions weren't always right; some of Sonny Boy's outtakes are legendary. He was still as contrary and devious as ever; he never did lose his taste for booze, gambling, or another man's woman. Eventually his health started to give out, and his success on records as well, but he got it all together in 1963 for one absolutely magnificent single called "Help Me."

He got to Europe a few times before he died, and recorded with The Animals and The Yardbirds. He had a London tailor make him an outrageously luxurious-looking suit to show off to the folks back home in Helena, who refused to believe he had become a worldwide celebrity. He hosted King Biscuit Time one last time before he was found dead in his bed on May 25, 1965.

Sonny Boy left behind some wonderful songs—"Nine Below Zero," "One Way Out" and "Help Me" are among his standards. Many think Sonny Boy was an even better harmonica player than Little Walter, and his influence on blues harp today is second only to Walter's. He had total command of the instrument: he could even play a decent solo with the entire harmonica stuffed inside his mouth.

BLUES & BOOZE
(and other drugs)...

Wherever blues is performed—from the roughest Mississippi juke joint to the ritziest Beverly Hills cocktail lounge, from the toughest ghetto bar to the friendliest outdoor blues festival—you'll generally find people consuming alcohol. Blues and booze just seem to go together.

Even for people who don't drink much, there's something about blues that blends nicely with a beer or two…its simple, comfortable and familiar form; its repetitious patterns; and perhaps most of all, its emotional openness. It's no accident that so many local pubs have one or more Blues Nights every week.

For many, of course, the influence of alcohol has been far less benign. Many a bluesman's career has been cut short by alcohol's effects. Little Walter, dead at age 38. Blind Boy Fuller, 33. Guitar Slim, 32. Leroy Carr, 30. To that dolorous list you might also add Robert Johnson, dead at 27 after drinking poisoned whiskey, or Pine Top Smith, only 25 when he caught a stray bullet in a speakeasy gunfight. Many others who lived longer were also severely affected by alcoholism—T-Bone Walker, Son House, Wynonie Harris. Tommy Johnson craved alcohol so much that he'd eat Sterno—the cooking fuel called "canned heat"—

to get the alcohol it contained. He sang a fine blues about it, and the band Canned Heat took their name from that song. Tommy McClennan sang "Whiskey Head Man," Bessie Smith "Me And My Gin," Robert Johnson "Drunken Hearted Man," Tampa Red "Drinkin' My Blues Away," Muddy Waters "Sittin' Here and Drinkin'," Leroy Carr (and many others since) "Sloppy Drunk Blues" ("I would rather be sloppy drunk than anything I know".) Amos Milburn had a song for every bottle in the bar.

There was no lack of awareness that booze was not always the drinker's friend: Blind Blake sang "Fightin' the Jug." Peetie Wheatstraw sang "Drinking Man Blues."

That stuff will kill you, but it just won't quit
  (twice)
It will get you to the place, ooh well well, that
  you don't care who you hit.
I been drinking that stuff, and it went to my
  head (twice)
It made me hit the baby in the cradle, oooh,
  well, well, and kill my papa dead.

Big Bill Broonzy, not remembered as a man with a drinking problem, sang "Good Liquor Gonna Carry Me Down."

Lord, I knowed a little girl 'bout sixteen years
*   old*
She says 'Bill, stop drinkin' and I will satisfy
*   your soul'*
But I just keep on a-drinkin', yes, I keep on
*   drinkin'*
Yeah, I just keep on a-drinkin' till good liquor
*   carry me down.*

Lord, I woke up this mornin' holdin' a bottle
*   tight*
When I lay down at night, mama, just a gallon
*   out of sight*
But I just keep on a-drinkin', etc.

Lord, my woman told me to stop drinkin' and
*   come on home*
Say, if you don't, Big Bill, some other man gonna
*   carry your business on*
But I just keep on a-drinkin', etc.

Things have changed in recent decades. Naturally, the older bluesmen who are still with us tend to be the ones less addicted to alcohol than their departed contemporaries, and their example has been meaningful. B.B. King, who knocked back a few early in his career, has often spoken of how much better off he's been since he gave up the sauce. For those who make the decision that they would be better off without alcohol, many resources are available (such as AA) that earlier bluesmen simply did not have access to.

♦

Through the entire history of blues, other drugs besides alcohol have also been available, but in the words of researcher Paul Garon, "The large number of references to alcohol in the blues, and there are hundreds, throws into stark contrast the relatively few mentions of other drugs: heroin, marihuana, and cocaine" (Paul Garon, *Blues and the Poetic Spirit*, p. 94).

In 1930 the Memphis Jug Band offered "Cocaine Habit Blues," better known as "Take A Whiff On Me."

Cocaine habit is mighty bad, worst old habit I
*   ever had*
Hey hey, honey take a whiff on me…
I love my whiskey, love my gin, but the way I
*   love my coke is a doggone sin*
Hey hey, honey take a whiff on me…

A few years later, Leadbelly sang a version with these lines:

Walked down Ellum and I come down Main,
*   tryin' to bum a nickel just to buy cocaine,*
Oh, baby take a whiff on me…

Cocaine's for horses, not for men, doctor says it
  kill you but he don't say when,
Oh, baby take a whiff on me.

Victoria Spivey was presumably referring to cocaine when she sang "Dope Head Blues" in 1927...

Just give me one more sniffle, another sniffle
  of that dope
Just give me one more sniffle, another sniffle
  of that dope
I'll catch a cow like a cowboy, and throw a bull
  without a rope.

Marijuana is notable for its utter absence from pre-WWII rural blues, but it was popular with jazzmen from the start (Louis Armstrong was a thorough devotee) and it pops up now and then in 1930s urban blues of the jazzier variety, such as Rosetta Howard's colorful "If You're a Viper," recorded with the Harlem Hamfats:

Dreamed about a reefer five feet long,
Mighty mezz but not too strong,
You'll be high, but not for long,
  If you're a viper...
When your throat gets dry, you know you're
  high,
Everything is dandy.
Truck on down to the candy store,
Bust your conk on peppermint candy...

Heroin was also a presence in the jazz world, but one that few blues singers paid heed to.

The Memphis Jug Band's "Cocaine Habit" did contain this line:

Since cocaine went out of style, you can catch
  'em shootin' needles all the while...
Hey hey, honey take a whiff on me...

Champion Jack Dupree was the only veteran bluesman to broach the subject at any greater length on records, in his 1941 "Junker Blues" and a few later pieces.

It wasn't until the 1960s that heroin, cocaine and the like became a scourge in the blues world. And when they did, it was mainly younger white bluesmen who were affected: Paul Butterfield, Mike Bloomfield, Bob Hite, Eric Clapton, Stevie Ray Vaughan. These were people from the same milieu as rock musicians, and we know only too well the heavy toll that drugs have exacted on the rock music world. Many of these young artists were alcoholics as well.

Blues today, like blues in 1900, is a reflection of the society in which it lives. Now that blues has gained a measure of middle-class respectability it never knew before, and an awareness of political correctness that goes with it, explicit references to alcohol and other drugs are less often heard in new blues lyrics than they used to be, though such old favorites as "One Scotch, One Bourbon, One Beer" are still sung with feeling.

Chapter 7

Chicago Electric

As mentioned earlier, Lester Melrose produced countless blues sessions after the war. Sonny Boy Williamson (#1) just kept getting better until his tragic death in 1948. He showed the world how to do country blues with a rhythm section. Sonny Boy also guested on some excellent 1947 Columbia sides by Big Joe Williams, including a new version of "Baby, Please Don't Go."

Arthur (Big Boy) Crudup (1905-1974) was Melrose's new guitar blues star of the 1940s. Crudup moved from Mississippi to Chicago in 1939 and was singing on the streets when Melrose found him. A limited though forceful singer and guitarist, he was a fine songwriter. "Mean Old Frisco" quickly became a standard, and "So Glad You're Mine" is another winner, but Arthur Crudup will forever be best known as the man whose 1946 B-side inspired Elvis Presley's very first record release—"That's All Right."

ARTHUR "BIG BOY" CRUDUP

THAT'S ALL RIGHT MAMA
(RCA 61043)
An excellent selection of his best and most popular work.

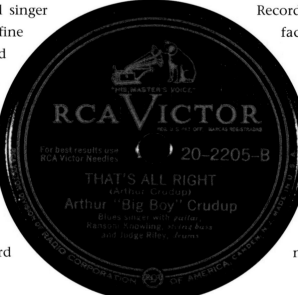

Melrose's hottest ticket for a while was the **Big Three Trio**, which played boogie instrumentals featuring pianist Leonard Caston, and sang blues and novelty numbers in unique three-part harmony featuring the deep voice of Willie Dixon—the same Willie Dixon who would go on to be Chess Records' studio bassist, and the de facto producer of some of the greatest blues of the 1950s.

Overall, Melrose's efforts yielded steadily diminishing returns. In 1946, he and Columbia Records let the biggest prize in all Chicago slip through their fingers...a singer-guitarist from the Mississippi Delta who went by the name of Muddy Waters.

WILLIE DIXON

THE BIG THREE TRIO

(Columbia CK 46216)
This otherwise fine compilation oddly omits the group's signature song, "You Sure Look Good To Me."

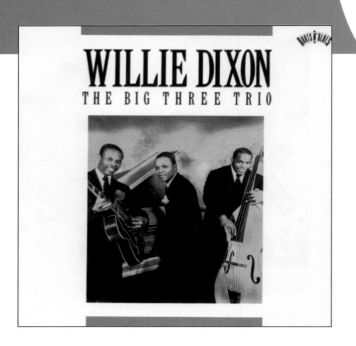

Muddy

Muddy Waters (McKinley Morganfield, 1915-1983) would go on to be the world's most celebrated living bluesman, renowned as the chief architect of a then-revolutionary style of blues that profoundly influenced a generation of rockers.

We call that blues Chicago Electric, because it first surfaced in Chicago and because it stood out from other blues at first for its emphasis on electronic amplification. It wasn't the first electric blues; T-Bone Walker had been plugging in for a decade before the Chicago sound got started. The difference was that while T-Bone's tone was smooth and silky (at least on records), Muddy Waters cranked up his amp until the electronic circuitry was overworked and the sound was distorted. It was intense, it was in your face—just like the blues of the Delta where Muddy came from.

People soon grew to love that sound, and demand it. Decades later, rock guitarists would spend fortunes on state-of-the-art gear modified to sound just like that primitive amp that Muddy had…but we get ahead of ourselves.

Muddy was born into a sharecropping family near Clarksdale, and raised by his grandmother after his mother died when he was three. He got his life-long nickname because he liked to play in a muddy creek nearby. He began playing (acoustic) guitar in his late teens, inspired by the deep blues of local favorite Son House. Robert Johnson (four years Muddy's senior) was also in the neighborhood from time to time, and Muddy felt his influence too.

Muddy was 26 years old and sharecropping eight acres on Sherrod's plantation when folksong collector Alan Lomax came through on one of his Library of

Congress expeditions in the summer of 1941. Lomax was blown away by his blues, by the skill of his slide guitar playing and the poetry of his lyrics. He came back for more the next year, recording him solo and a member of The Son Simms Four, a little band led by a fiddler who had recorded with Charlie Patton 12 years earier. Two of the solo pieces, "Country Blues" and "I Be's Troubled," were included in a non-commercial record album of music by various Lomax discoveries that was made available to libraries and scholars in 1942. (Lomax describes his encounters with Muddy in his book *The Land Where the Blues Began*.)

That helped convince Muddy that he might be able to make a living from his music. He definitely wasn't making one from sharecropping, so he lit out for Chicago in 1943. He quickly fell in with the cadre of musicians who had been making records for Lester Melrose. For a while he played acoustic guitar behind Sonny Boy Willamson (#1). In 1944 he began playing electric guitar.

With the recording scene hamstrung by the musician's union strike and the shellac shortage, Waters didn't get his chance to record for Melrose until a 1946 session for Columbia Records.

The Columbia bigwigs heard Muddy's efforts—and decided they weren't worth releasing. While it would make a nice story to say Muddy's blues was too loud and intense for them, that proved not to be the case when the tracks saw the light of day 25 years later. Muddy sings his heart out, and plays some of his signature licks on electric guitar…but the guitar is buried behind Sunnyland Slim's 1930s urban piano playing. (Slim was a fine pianist, but the chemistry just didn't work that day.) Worse, the music has a stiff, plodding beat. It just isn't great blues.

Whatever may have gone wrong that day, Slim soon did Muddy a giant favor by recommending him to one of those new record labels that started at the end of the war, Aristocrat Records. His first session, with Slim, was an improvement on the Columbias, and "Gypsy Woman" was released (with the artist credited as "Muddy Water") to modest local response. Aristocrat was ready to drop him, but decided one day in April 1948 to try Muddy with just his cranked-up guitar and a standup bass, doing the same two songs Alan Lomax had selected for that Library of Congress album six years earlier, retitled "I Feel Like Going Home" and "I Can't Be Satisfied."

This was the record Chicago's fast-growing community of ex-Mississippians had been waiting for. It was pure down-home music, but with an urban edge from the electricity and from Muddy's newly energized singing. It sold out overnight, and soon became a national R&B hit as well, the first ever for Aristocrat as well as for Muddy.

The record made Muddy a star on the local nightclub scene, and soon he began assembling a band to play the blues his way. But the record company didn't want to mess with success, and insisted that Muddy record with only his guitar and the bass for a while. Among his "solo" sides were such wonders as the old Delta stardard "Rollin' and Tumblin'," Robert Johnson's "Walkin' Blues" (ultimately derived from Son House), and "Rollin' Stone," after which a certain British band named itself a decade later. The full band didn't make it to the studios until 1952, but Muddy was able to bring in his sidemen one or two at a time.

Before we get to those sidemen, a word about the record company. Aristocrat was founded in 1946, and recorded a variety of Chicago music—pop, country, jump blues—without much success until Muddy came along. Among its partners were Leonard and Phil Chess, Polish immigrants who had been introduced to blues through some bars and taverns that they opened in Chicago's black neighborhoods. After Muddy's success, the Chess brothers bought out their partners and re-named the label Chess—a name that became synonymous with the Chicago electric sound, and the most revered record label in all postwar blues history.

Muddy picked his sidemen with uncommon skill, as he developed the most intense and forceful blues band sound ever heard up to that point. Many of his musicians became stars on their own either while working with him or afterward: harmonica players Little Walter and Junior Wells, guitarist Jimmy Rogers, pianist Otis Spann, bassist Willie Dixon. (More on each of them shortly.) As the band sound got even tighter and stronger in the mid-1950s, Muddy cut back on his guitar playing and concentrated on his singing. Just as B. B. King brought some of his gospel singing style to blues, Muddy brought back the voice of the country preacher he had briefly been back in Mississippi. He became the ultimate personification of blues macho, roaring his way through hits like "I'm Ready," "I Just Want To Make Love To You" and "She's Nineteen Years Old."

Like B.B., Muddy felt his core audience aging and shrinking a bit as the 1960s arrived. However, he was beginning to win himself a new audience—younger, and predominantly white. One turning point was a 1960 appearance at the Newport Jazz Festival in Rhode Island, where he turned the song "Got My Mojo Working" (a so-so seller for him in 1957) into an old-time sanctified shout. A live album of the show opened a lot of new doors for Muddy.

Chess Records didn't always have a handle on how to handle Muddy's new audience. They packaged him as a folksinger, then as a rocker in a series of misbegotten albums. Fortunately Chess also com-

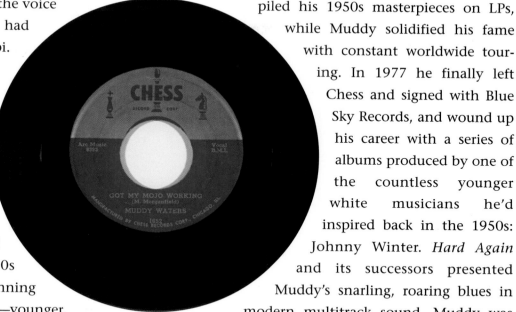

piled his 1950s masterpieces on LPs, while Muddy solidified his fame with constant worldwide touring. In 1977 he finally left Chess and signed with Blue Sky Records, and wound up his career with a series of albums produced by one of the countless younger white musicians he'd inspired back in the 1950s: Johnny Winter. *Hard Again* and its successors presented Muddy's snarling, roaring blues in modern multitrack sound. Muddy was back at the top of his game when he died of a heart attack in his sleep at age 68.

Muddy's Men

Harmonica player **Little Walter** (Marion Walter Jacobs, 1930-1968) was Muddy's best-known sideman, and a giant in his own right...the most influential harmonica man blues has ever known. His aim was to make a five-dollar harmonica sound like Count Basie's big band. What he wound up

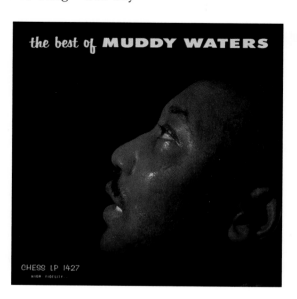

MUDDY WATERS

THE CHESS BOX

(MCA-Chess CHD3-80002)
Three CDs with most of his best up to 1972.

HARD AGAIN

(Blue Sky 34449)
The comeback with Johnny Winter.

THE COMPLETE PLANTATION RECORDINGS—HISTORIC 1941–42 LIBRARY OF CONGRESS FIELD RECORDINGS

(MCA Chess 9344)
Where it all began.

doing was to make a whole new instrument out of it. He would take that little ten-hole harmonica and a cheap microphone (like the ones used to page people in factories), hold them against each other, cup his hands around them both and blow. The distortion produced by the overloaded mike and the overloaded amp became part of his one-man orchestra. He made every note count, rhythmically as well as melodically. And when he switched, on occasion, to the larger chromatic harmonica, the sound was almost symphonic.

Walter was born in rural Louisiana but grew up mostly on city streets: New Orleans, St. Louis, then Chicago where he arrived about 1946. He made a record for the tiny Ora Nelle label the next year, but his career really began when Muddy Waters asked him to join his band a year later; Walter was 18. He began showing up on Muddy's records in 1950, unamplified at first.

For decades, blues bands have begun their live sets with an instrumental. On May 12, 1952, Chess Records decided to record one of Muddy's set-openers, featuring Little Walter's harp. It was titled "Juke," released under Walter's name…and became a nationwide smash hit, reaching #1 on the R&B charts, a distinction Muddy himself never managed in his entire career. Of course Walter immediately left Muddy and took his own band on the road. Actually, he took over rival harpist Junior Wells' band when Wells replaced him in Muddy's band. (Chess insisted that he continue to play harp on Muddy's records.) A goodly string of hits followed, including another #1 in 1955 with "My Babe."

Pretty soon, most every harmonica player in Chicago started cupping his hands like he did; to this day that's the way you most often hear harmonica in an electric blues band. Though nobody ever topped Walter, some came close enough that it takes a lot of expertise and experience to tell them apart on record.

Like Muddy, Walter found some European fame; he toured England with the Rolling Stones in 1964. Alas, he'd become a Grade-A lush by this time, and a nasty drunk too; he died of a blood clot to the brain after a Chicago street brawl at age 38. His harmonica work continues to inspire anyone who's ever picked up the instrument or enjoyed electric blues. Practically every note he ever blew in a studio has been put out on CD, outtakes and all, the sort of treatment given to jazz legends like Charlie Parker.

A little more about Walter's own sidemen. Brothers Louis and David Myers and drummer Fred Below were known as the Aces when they played with Junior Wells; with Walter they became the Night Cats and then the Jukes. They were all about Walter's age, and played with a more aggressive attack and often at faster tempos than Muddy's band did, kicking the Chicago blues further into the modern era. Many of Walter's records also featured guitarist Robert Jr. Lockwood.

LITTLE WALTER

THE ESSENTIAL LITTLE WALTER

(MCA-Chess CHD2-9342)
A 2-CD set with most of what made the man a legend (along with his work with Muddy, of course).

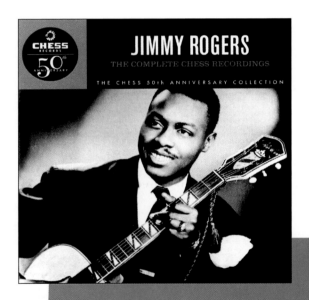

JIMMY ROGERS

THE COMPLETE CHESS RECORDINGS

(MCA Chess 9372)

Jimmy Rogers (1924-1997) was Muddy's backup guitarist until 1955. Though he was always somewhat in Waters' shadow he had a couple of big hits on his own, "That's All Right" (1950—a slow blues, not the Arthur Crudup song that Elvis recorded) and "Walking By Myself" (1956). His roots are in 1930s-style urban blues, and he remained a little closer to that style than Muddy was. After retiring from music for awhile, Rogers returned in the 1970s and enjoyed a solid career on revival stages in the USA and Europe until his death.

Otis Spann (1930-1970) joined Waters' band on piano in 1953 and immediately took its sound from great to stupendous. Though skilled in the same urban blues and boogie woogie patterns used by predecessors

OTIS SPANN

OTIS SPANN IS THE BLUES

(Candid 79001)
Often hailed as one of the best blues LPs of the 1960s, now on CD. With Robert Jr. Lockwood on guitar.

like Sunnyland Slim, Spann was much more flexible. He could make the rhythm section cook with simple riffs without trying to dominate it, then play a wonderful solo, plain or fancy as the occasion demanded. In the 1960s he recorded and toured as a singer-pianist with his own group. He died of cancer at age 40.

Willie Dixon (1915-1992) was Muddy's bass player and a whole lot more. He wrote many of Chess Records' biggest hits—"I Just Want To Make Love To You" and "I'm Your Hoochie Coochie Man" for Muddy, "My Babe" for Little Walter, "Spoonful, "Back Door Man" and "Little Red Rooster" for Howlin' Wolf. (His well-crafted songs have had a special attraction for rock bands like the Stones and Led Zeppelin.) He also did the informal unwritten arrangements for these and many other Chess blues recordings. The man had a special knack for little touches that gave electric blues more popular appeal without sacrificing its essence—in other words, he was a master of "hooks."

A big man, Willie was a heavyweight boxer for a little while before he became a blues heavyweight. After that, he lent his bass voice and his developing arranging skills to several vocal harmony groups, the last and most popular of which was the aforementioned Big Three Trio. He also spent some time behind bars, as a conscientious objector during World War II.

As his Chess activities started winding down, Willie devoted more attention to his singing career. Though he made a few fine albums, his greatest impact was as a statesman for the blues. In 1982, after winning a long fight to claim a fair share of royalties from his many hits, he used the money to start the Blues Heaven Foundation which continues a variety of good works, from promoting blues in the schools to assisting needy bluesmen.

✦

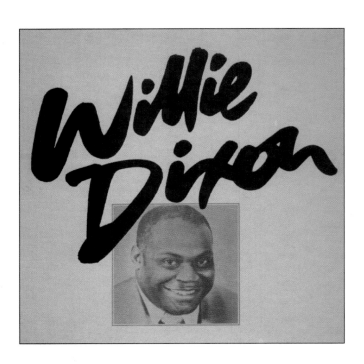

WILLIE DIXON

THE CHESS BOX

(MCA Chess 16500)
An enlightening 2-CD showcase of his songwriting and producing skills featuring most of the great Chess stars plus six vocals by Willie himself.

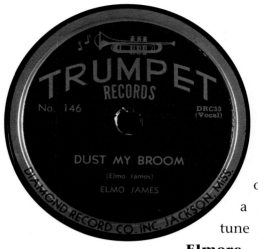

Muddy wasn't the only Delta-style singer-guitarist on the Chicago electric scene, or the only one to make a Robert Johnson tune famous. In fact, **Elmore James** (1918-1963) took a Johnson song and made it into the single most familiar song in all of electric blues, and quite possibly the single most-played blues song of the late 20th century: "Dust My Broom." The opening slide-guitar line never fails to get an audience on its feet.

James actually began his recording career in the South, where he is remembered as a street singer around the Delta town of Belzoni in the late 1930s, working the same territory as Sonny Boy Williamson #2. He undoubtedly met and played with Robert Johnson on one or more occasions. He cut his first version of "Dust My Broom" in 1952 for Trumpet Records in Jackson, Miss., with Williamson on harp, before moving to Chicago. Though a rather inordinate number of his subsequent records are thinly disguised remakes of "Dust My Broom," he also gave us such standards-to-be as "The Sky Is Crying," "Done Somebody Wrong," and "It Hurts Me Too" (the last a reworking of a Tampa Red song).

Unlike other electric Chicagoans, Elmore usually used a saxophone in his band. It worked just fine for him. His last few sessions, done in New York, were

ELMORE JAMES

THE SKY IS CRYING: THE HISTORY OF ELMORE JAMES

(Rhino 71190)

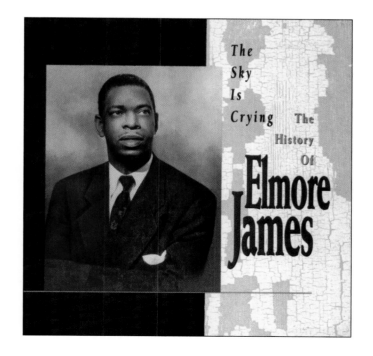

as up-to-date as blues got in the early 1960s. He undoubtedly would have connected very well with the emerging white blues fandom if he hadn't had a sudden massive heart attack on May 24, 1963, at age 45, in the Chicago apartment of his cousin "Homesick" James (Williamson), also a bluesman of some note.

The Wolf

Another man who began his career in the South and went on to much greatness in Chicago was the mighty **Howlin' Wolf** (Chester Arthur Burnett, 1910-1976). (Small wonder that a man named after our 21st president would prefer to be known by a nickname.)

Howlin' Wolf scared people. He still does. He grew up in the Mississippi Delta not far from where Charlie Patton lived. Wolf learned to perform by watching Charlie, and sang with a similar mixture of howl, roar and snarl. Not only that, he sang like a man possessed, which he probably was, leaping in the air or rolling on the floor as his spirit dictated. And not only that, he was more than twice the size of Charlie Patton—6'4", and "three hundred pounds of joy" as a song Willie Dixon wrote for him put it.

In the 1930s he met and played with Sonny Boy Williamson (#2), who taught him harmonica and married his sister, and Robert Johnson. However, he remained only a part-time musician (he was a full-time farmhand) until after World War II (he served with the Army in Seattle). In 1948 he formed his first band in West Memphis, Ark., and got some airtime on one of the several local stations that offered live blues (a phenomenon unique at the time to Memphis and eastern Arkansas). Local bandleader/talent scout Ike Turner (later of Ike & Tina fame) recommended him to local record man Sam Phillips (later of Sun Records/Elvis fame), who recorded Wolf at the future Sun Studios in Memphis in 1951 and leased the results to Chess.

The results turned out to be a two-sided national Top Ten R&B hit, "Moanin' at Midnight"/"How Many More Years." Phillips leased some more material from this period to RPM (the label B.B. King was on), and quite a bit more has appeared on CD recently, but Wolf's future was on Chess. He soon moved to Chicago and commenced a long and glorious series of Chess releases, including "Smoke Stack Lightning" (1956) and an especially brilliant run in the early 1960s: "Wang Dang Doodle," "Back Door Man," "Spoonful," "Down In the Bottom," "(Little) Red Rooster," "Built For Comfort." Though Willie Dixon and other Chess regulars often played along, Wolf's band had its own guitar star in Hubert Sumlin, who later launched a solo career.

Chess tried to market Wolf as a rocker in the 1960s, as the label did with Muddy.

HOWLIN' WOLF

THE CHESS BOX

(MCA-Chess CHC3-9332)
A definitive 3-CD retrospective.

He recorded with Eric Clapton and various Rolling Stones. Alas, he wasn't quite the wild man he'd once been, due to health problems (especially after a 1970 auto accident damaged his kidneys). We can get a small but stunning glimpse of what he was by hearing his CDs, especially the Chess sessions from 1951 to 1963.

The early 1950s Chicago scene included several other singers and players who'd learned their craft before World War II.

Big Walter ("Shakey") Horton (1917-1981) played harmonica with the Memphis Jug Band in the 1920s, then dropped out of sight only to pop up in the very midst of electric Chicago a quarter century later, wailing electric harmonica with Muddy Waters' band. He played and/or recorded with practically every bluesman in town in the late 1950s and 1960s, and stayed active until his death in 1981.

Robert Nighthawk (Robert Lee McCollum, 1909-1967) played and recorded from the mid-1930s to the mid-1960s without ever finding fame or fortune, but left behind some haunting vocals and unique single-string slide guitar work (you could call it a down-home Delta version of Tampa Red's "Hawaiian" style).

Johnny Shines (1915-1992) was a Delta singer and slide guitarist who made a few nice records in Chicago around 1950 ("Ramblin'" was the pick of the litter) but was elbowed aside because he didn't fit into the emerging electric band sound. Then, in the 1960s, researchers discovered that he'd spent a lot of time in the 1930s playing and travelling with Robert Johnson. Though he never played or sang much *like* Johnson, that was enough to make him a club, concert and festival attraction for the rest of his life.

Robert "Jr." Lockwood (1915-   ) has even closer ties to Johnson. Along with teaching Lockwood to play, Johnson married his mother! (Thus the "Junior.") He also played and travelled a lot with Sonny Boy Williamson (#2). He recorded four tracks for Lester Melrose in 1941 in a thoroughly Johnsonian style. After that he got into jazz, which served him well when he showed up in Chicago around 1950. Unlike Shines he caught on nicely as an electric blues sideman, playing nice jazz chords along with standard blues patterns on many records by Little Walter and Sonny Boy Williamson #2. He eventually relocated to Cleveland and became the honored dean of that city's blues scene, while continuing to tour and record.

The Next Generation

Most of the other Chicago stars were born in the 1920s and '30s, and made their reputation while in *their* 20s and 30s. We've already mentioned singer-harmonica player **Junior Wells** (b. Amos Blakemore, 1934-1998). He was still in his mid-teens when his band, The Aces, became Muddy Waters' first real rival on the Chicago scene, and only 18 when he replaced Little Walter in Muddy's band in 1952, while the remaining Aces hit the road with Walter. In 1953

JUNIOR WELLS

1957-1963: MESSIN' WITH THE KID

(Paula 03)

HOODOO MAN BLUES

(Delmark 612)
One of the very first electric blues albums made for the revival audience.

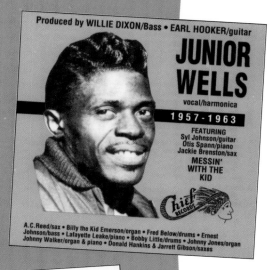

he began recording under his own name and over the next decade produced such hot local hits as "Somebody Hoodooed the Hoodoo Man," "Messin' With the Kid" and "Little By Little." A 1966 LP called *Hoodoo Man Blues* introduced him to the rest of the world. In 1970 he toured Europe with the Rolling Stones. He continued to delight revival audiences worldwide until his death in 1998.

James Cotton (1935-) got harmonica lessons from Sonny Boy Williamson (#2) while still a youngster in the 1940s. At 17 he recorded with Howlin' Wolf in Memphis. At 20 he joined Muddy Waters' band and stayed with him for a decade, appearing on many records with "Rock Me" (1957) a particular standout. Cotton continues to keep the Chicago Electric sound alive and well.

JAMES COTTON

LIVING THE BLUES

(Gitanes-Verve 314 521 238)
The harp master's contemporary sound.

CHESS CASHES IN: Chuck and Bo

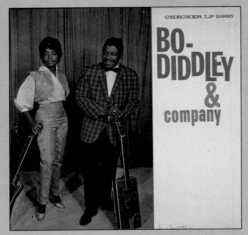

Chuck Berry and Bo Diddley may be rockers more than bluesmen…but both grew up with blues. You can hear strains of blues in all of their work, and they've each headlined blues festivals in recent years. In mid-1955 each of them put Chess Records high on the nationwide charts with his first release.

Bo Diddley (Otha Ellas Bates McDaniels, 1928-) came first, with his two-sided smash "Bo Did-dley"/"I'm a Man" on Chess' Checker label. Both songs were incredibly influential, especially the song Bo named after himself, with its "shave-and-a-hair-cut—six bits" rhythm (known ever after as the "Bo Diddley beat"—Bo claimed he was inspired by some African rhythms in an unidentified movie) and its lyrics lifted from ancient childrens' rhymes.

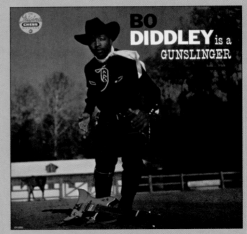

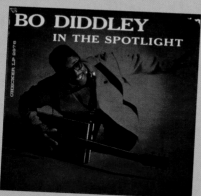

Bo was born in Mississippi and raised in Chicago. In the late 1940s he started making music on Chicago street corners with his friend Jerome Green, who appears on most of Bo's 1950s classics as maracas player and/or comedy foil. Soon he was making waves on the club scene with his macho moves and his guitar (always cranked up to 10 plus, often played through a tremolo device synchonized with the song's rhythm). People called it "jun-

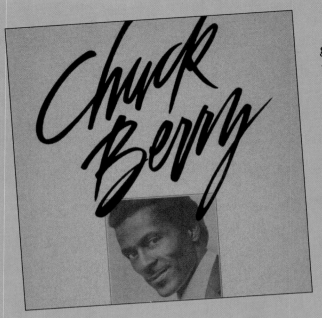

gle music." Square guitars and other crazy shapes soon became part of the act. After the hit singles petered out, his LPs remained frat-party faves well into the 1960s. Oldies shows helped keep him going until his most recent big break—a Nike TV commercial featuring Bo along with Bo Jackson, the athlete.

Chuck Berry (1926-) grew up in St. Louis, and began his professional career in a trio which played a remarkable mixture of jazz, pop, blues and country music. While in Chicago seeking a record deal, he got Muddy Waters to recommend him to Chess. His first record, "Maybellene," had a little jazz and a lot of blues and country in it, plus Willie Dixon on bass. It became Chess' first crossover pop hit, the first of dozens for Berry, most of which feature Dixon and other Chess studio regulars in the band.

Chuck Berry is rightly regarded as one of the founders of the rock 'n' roll dynasty, one of its finest guitarists, one of its greatest songwriters, and one of its top showmen, with the duck walk and all. His occasional collisions with the authorities have only added to the legend.

CHUCK BERRY
THE CHESS BOX

(Chess CHD3-80,001)
As many hits as 3 CDs can hold.

BO DIDDLEY
THE CHESS BOX

(Chess CHD2-19502)
All the 1950s hit singles plus a nice selection of 1960s album tracks, on 2 CDs.

The Boogie Man

Like Chicago, the city of Detroit attracted many African-American migrants from Mississippi in the 1940s. But though Berry Gordy Jr. and Motown Records put the city on the music map starting in the late 1950s, there wasn't much recording done in Detroit before that, which explains why most of the bluesmen went to Chicago instead.

The Detroit scene did give us one titanic blues-man: **John Lee Hooker** (1915-). No one has ever sung or played blues that cut deeper than John Lee Hooker's best. His deep, dark voice and pungent guitar style are instantly recognizable. Even his lesser recordings, like the guest star–glutted affairs released in the 1990s, leave an unforgettable impression.

Hooker was born in Clarksdale, Mississippi, and also lived in Memphis and Cincinnati before arriving in Detroit in 1943 to work in an auto plant. He'd been a part-time bluesman since his teens, and had also sung in several gospel quartets, without ever getting a chance to record. After playing around Detroit for a few years he attracted the attention of Bernie Besman, who ran a small local label and also leased recordings to labels elsewhere. Besman leased Hooker's first-ever recordings to the Modern label of Los Angeles, which released "Boogie Chillen'" at the end of 1948.

Out of nowhere, he had the hottest R&B record in the country. Small bands were making most of the R&B noise then, but here was one man, one guitar, doing it all. And it wasn't even an electric guitar, but a standard acoustic run through a special echo chamber Bernie Besman had rigged up. It sounded cranked, but there was a crisper top end than the amps of those

**JOHN LEE HOOKER
THE ULTIMATE
COLLECTION**

(Rhino R2-70252)
You're likely to find more different CDs by John Lee Hooker in your local store than by any other blues artist. Some are great, some aren't. This 2-CD compilation, spanning his whole career to date, is the one to start with.

days could manage. The beat was irresistible, and the voice hit home. (He did use an electric for live appearances.)

Hooker had a lot more songs where "Boogie Chillen" came from, and he recorded all of them. When one label had enough masters to last awhile, he went across the street and recorded some more for someone else. To avoid lawsuits they came out under different names: Texas Slim, Johnny Williams, The Boogie Man, Birmingham Sam and his Magic Guitar, not to mention John Lee Booker and plain John Lee. But there was no mistaking the man, even when the tapes were sped up a notch or two. He did save another #1 R&B hit, "I'm In The Mood," for Modern Records.

In the 1950s he often recorded with bands. Some of these are splendid, like "Dimples" and "Boom Boom" (the latter became a smash for The Animals); others are exercises in chaos. Some are terrific songs; others are half-baked improvisations. In 1959 he tried a different approach, recording an LP for the white folk audience on the Riverside label, using an unamplified acoustic guitar and singing some of the oldest songs he knew (rather than making up his own as he usually did). From that point on he seemed equally at home with the acoustic and electric version of himself. In the 1960s he had a full schedule of gigs on both sides of the Atlantic.

In 1970 he recorded a double LP with Canned Heat, a band of young white musicians that had partly modelled itself on Hooker's boogie style. *Hooker 'n Heat* remains one of blues' more successful cross-generational projects. Not much he recorded after that is comparable to his earlier work, but then, what is?! Hooker has settled nicely into his role as a revered elder of the blues. Hopefully the money he's made from TV commercials has made up for some of the dues he had to pay on his way there.

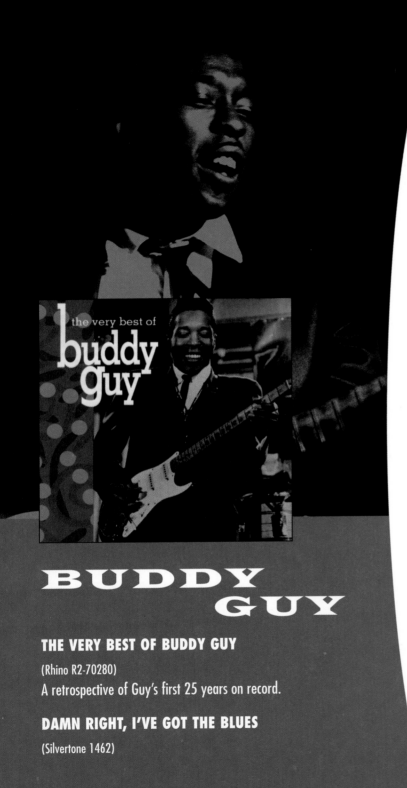

BUDDY GUY

THE VERY BEST OF BUDDY GUY

(Rhino R2-70280)
A retrospective of Guy's first 25 years on record.

DAMN RIGHT, I'VE GOT THE BLUES

(Silvertone 1462)

The guitar player on Junior Wells' *Hoodoo Man Blues* went on to work with Wells for many years around the world and on records. Decades of mercurial live shows eventually made **Buddy Guy** (b. George Guy, 1936-) the best-known active veteran of the 1950s Chicago scene. He began his career in Baton Rouge, La., in his late teens, then moved to Chicago in 1957. By that time, newer (and poorer) African-American migrants from the South were clustering on Chicago's West Side, a few miles from the original black ghetto on the South Side. The new "West Side Sound" was closer to B.B. King than to Muddy Waters, with its gospel-tinged singing and single-string guitar solos, but it still had the heat and speed that was all Chicago. The 21-year-old Guy quickly got a reputation as one of the most exciting West Side performers and soon began recording both as a singer and as a side-man for Waters, Koko Taylor and other Chess Records stars. From the mid-1960s on he performed and toured almost constantly, often with Wells. A series of 1991 shows in London with Eric Clapton attracted much attention and led to a new record deal with the Silvertone label. These CDs, with cameos from Clapton, Mark Knopfler et al., are among the most celebrated blues discs of the 1990s.

Magic Sam (Sam Maghett, 1937-1969) might have been the best of all the young West Side singer-guitarists. Born in the Mississippi Delta town of Grenada, he moved to Chicago in his teens. He began recording in 1957 and ran

MAGIC SAM

WEST SIDE GUITAR
(Paula 02)
His 1950s singles.

WEST SIDE SOUL
(Delmark 615)

MAGIC SAM LIVE
(Delmark 645)

off a string of local hit singles, interrupted briefly when he was drafted (he went AWOL to make more records, and was briefly imprisoned before being discharged). In 1967 an LP called *West Side Soul* led to triumphal concert and festival appearances. Magic Sam was on the brink of great fame when he dropped dead one morning of a heart attack. He was only 32.

Otis Rush (1934-) was the first of the young West Siders to record, making the national R&B charts in 1956 with his first single, "I Can't Quit You Baby." A lefthanded guitarist, he's been a major inspiration to younger white blues players in particular; Stevie Ray Vaughan named his band after Otis' song "Double Trouble." A series of nightmarish experiences with record companies kept him from the recognition he deserved in the 1960s and early 1970s, but he came charging back in the 1990s with a fine album and a 1994 W.C. Handy Award as Male Blues Artist Of the Year.

Earl Hooker (1930-1970) played slide guitar on many of Junior Wells' early-1960s singles and on many other local 45s, including a few under his own name. He was born in Clarksdale, Miss., and raised in Chicago, where he went to music school and

OTIS RUSH

COBRA RECORDINGS

(Paula 01)
His tough and soulful songs from the 1950s.

AIN'T ENOUGH COMIN' IN

(Mercury 314 518 769)
The comeback album.

learned a variety of instruments. He began his professional career in Memphis before returning to the Windy City in the mid-1950s. In the mid-1960s he began recording LPs for the world market, often featuring a double-neck guitar. People were starting to call him the best slide guitarist ever to come out of Chicago when he died of tuberculosis at age 40.

Jimmy Reed

While Chicago blues continued to get harder, faster and more soulful in the late 1950s and early 1960s, there was one artist who bucked the trend in just about every conceivable way...and wound up selling more records during that time than all the West Siders put together, more even than Muddy Waters or Howlin' Wolf. His name was **Jimmy Reed** (1925-1976).

Whereas Muddy, Wolf and Buddy Guy got in your face, Jimmy Reed shyly but slyly seduced you with a laid-back groove (the same one on almost every song) and sang in a lazy drawl that was enhanced

EARL HOOKER

TWO BUGS AND A ROACH

(Arhoolie 324)

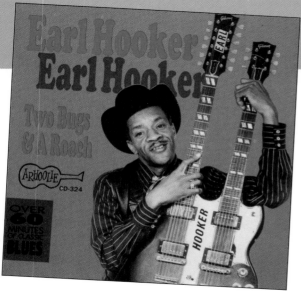

by a slight lisp. The longer Reed's string of hits continued, the mellower his grooves got.

He sang and played guitar *and* harmonica…the latter held with a brace like the one Bob Dylan wears. That meant no Little Walter orchestral effects with the cupped hands and all…just simple little harmonica lines in between the verses. He was very fond of the piercing notes on the high end of the harp. In its way, it was as distinctive a sound as Walter's.

Reed was born in Mississippi, moved North during World War II, and began playing Chicago clubs around 1949. After being turned down by Chess, he signed with Vee-Jay Records (a black-owned firm which became Chess' biggest rival on the Chicago scene) in 1953. He charted nationally in 1955 with his third release, "You Don't Have To Go," and again in 1956 with "Ain't That

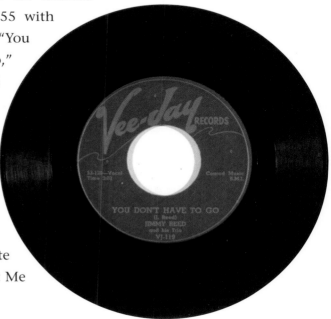

Lovin' You Baby." On those early hits he operated a little closer to the standard Chicago intensity level.

Two other people were very much a part of Reed's sound. Guitarist Eddie Taylor grew up with him in Mississippi and helped him create that easy groove in Chicago. Reed's wife "Mama" wrote many of the songs and can sometimes be heard softly singing along with Jimmy. She's quite audible on two of Reed's biggest hits, "Baby What You Want Me

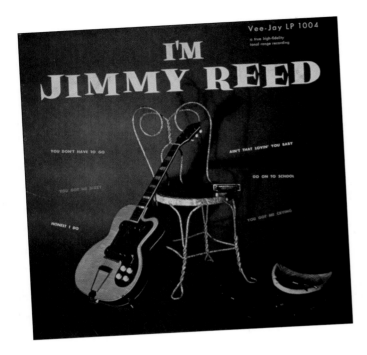

Vee-Jay LP 1004
a true high-fidelity
tonal range recording

I'M JIMMY REED

YOU DON'T HAVE TO GO

AIN'T THAT LOVIN' YOU BABY

YOU GOT ME DIZZY

GO ON TO SCHOOL

HONEST I DO

YOU GOT ME CRYING

To Do" (a.k.a. "You Got Me Runnin'," 1959) and "Bright Lights, Big City" (1961).

Vee-Jay began packaging his music on LPs in 1958, and while Muddy was courting folk and jazz

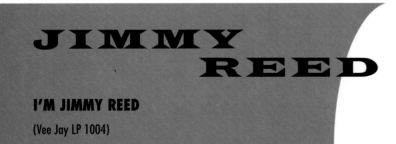

JIMMY REED

I'M JIMMY REED

(Vee Jay LP 1004)

audiences, Reed's LPs became favorites at college fraternity bashes. His music mixes extremely well with alcohol, after all. He consumed a great deal of it—"I was gluttin' just like it was a cool drink of water" he said after finally taking to the wagon. He also suffered from epilepsy, which did him in at age 51. But in the end, what matters most about Jimmy Reed is his songwriting—simple truths, succinctly and beautifully expressed.

Vee-Jay also had a bit of success with another harmonica man, **Billy Boy Arnold** (1935-), whose style most recalls Sonny Boy Williamson #1. His Vee-Jay singles included "I Wish You Would" and also "I Ain't Got You," later covered by the Yardbirds. He has continued to perform and record through the years.

Before leaving Chicago we should mention a few popular local artists who stayed a little closer to the 1930s urban piano blues than those we've mentioned. **Eddie Boyd** (1914-1994) was born in Clarksdale and began his career in Memphis. He made his first records with Lester Melrose in 1947 (as "Little Eddie Boyd") but broke through in 1952 on the tiny J.O.B. label with "Five Long Years," one of the biggest national R&B hits of that year. After the American hits stopped coming he found a warmer reception in Europe and eventually settled in Helsinki. His piano style is notable for its ringing pentatonic chords (which may remind you a bit of Native American music). **Willie Mabon** (1925-1985) was a bit closer to the West Coast jump sound. His biggest hit was "I Don't Know" (1952) with its colorful lyrics about a woman who, among other things, could throw a pile of clothes out the window and run outside and catch them before they fell. He, too, made it big in Europe later on. **J. B. Lenoir** (1929-1967) was noted for his natural high tenor voice (not a falsetto) and for songs of social commentary like "Eisenhower Blues" (1954) which was reputed to have gotten his record label in a heap of trouble. He remained popular in Chicago until the early 1960s, and was just hitting his stride in Europe when he died from the aftereffects of an auto accident back home, at age 38.

◆

As mentioned, the core audience for Chicago blues began to age and shrink in the 1960s. Electric Chicago had never been quite as big a deal commercially as one might think, considering its enormous influence on later generations, and the scene withered severely. Vee-Jay Records moved to Hollywood in the early 1960s and soon went broke (though not before temporarily landing the American rights to the Beatles' first album, and signing rocker Little Richard—whose band included a young Jimi Hendrix, who played a searing solo on one of Vee-Jay's last 45s). Chess gradually wound down, especially after Leonard Chess died in 1969.

Meanwhile, Delmark Records, a small label attached to a record store for blues and jazz buffs, made some of the first intelligently produced LPs of Chicago blues, packaged for a young international audience. A few clubs kept the blues and booze flowing through the lean years of the 1970s. In the mid-1980s, everything was re-energized as part of the worldwide blues revival. Today the city hosts a lively club scene, and the country's largest annual blues festival. Willie Dixon's Blues Heaven Foundation bought the old Chess Records building and turned it into a museum. The city's Establishment considers blues a matter of enormous civic pride…something that most definitely wasn't the case when Muddy and Wolf and Little Walter were first plugging in a half century ago!

Chapter 8
The South Rises Again

Prologue

While hundreds of thousands of African-Americans hit the road for Chicago and Los Angeles in the 1940s, others headed for the great cities of the South—Dallas, Houston, New Orleans.

New record companies sprang up in the South as they had elsewhere, and many recordings were also made there by new companies based elsewhere. Both urban and rural Southern blues were copiously recorded.

Texas provided us with a wealth of urban and rural blues alike. So did Memphis. New Orleans developed a style of its own; so did nearby Baton Rouge. Hundreds of singers made records all over the South, but most of the ones that became nationally known were centered in one of those places.

Texas

The first blues star to rise in the South after the war was Sam **"Lightnin'" Hopkins** (1912-1982). Like John Lee Hooker and Muddy Waters, he was a local entertainer whose first record releases appealed to record buyers all over the South. Hopkins actually hit the market first, in 1946.

Hopkins was born in Centerville, a small town halfway between Dallas and Houston. He was inspired to be a blues singer and guitarist after hearing and meeting Blind Lemon Jefferson as a boy. It happened that a cousin of Hopkins, Alger "Texas" Alexander, could sing rather like Jefferson but wasn't much of a guitarist. Young Sam Hopkins often accompanied him at country gatherings around East Texas in the late 1920s and early '30s. (Alexander made over 60 recordings during this period, but Hopkins is not known to have played on any of them; Lonnie Johnson and King Oliver were among Alexander's known accompanists.)

Both men apparently spent some time in prison after that, but they were singing again on the streets of Houston when Aladdin Records of Los Angeles came to town looking for blues talent. They passed on Alexander but signed Hopkins, along with a piano player, Wilson "Thunder" Smith. When they recorded together, Aladdin called them Thunder and Lightning.

You can hear Thunder on Lightnin's first hit, "Katie Mae," but the meteorological partnership didn't last long; Lightnin' sounded better without a pianist. Though Lightnin' was a much more laid-back stylist than Blind Lemon, the two rural Texans had one thing in common: they sang blues without much regard for the strict 12-bar chorus structure, letting guitar interludes between lines and verses go on as long as they felt right. That made things more difficult for backup musicians, of course.

Lightnin' didn't sound much like John Lee Hooker, either, but like Hooker he had a lot of songs to sing and was always making up more, and was eager to record them for whoever had a little money. Hopkins may well have made more records than any other blues singer, ever. This is remarkable partly because no single or album of his was ever a break-through best-seller, like Hooker's "Boogie Chillen."

LIGHTNIN' HOPKINS

MOJO HAND: THE LIGHTNIN' HOPKINS ANTHOLOGY

(Rhino R2-71226)
Two CDs spanning his entire recording career.

Most of them were just excellent blues that found a loyal audience.

Audiences were a little scarcer for Lightnin' in the 1950s, when singers with bands scored most of the hits. He didn't record from 1953 until 1959, when researcher Samuel Charters recorded an LP of him for the Folkways label, which made Lightnin's kinship with older blues traditions obvious. He was immediately welcomed by folk music fans, and performed at coffeehouses, concerts and festivals all over the U.S.A. in the 1960s, making his way to Europe as well. His recordings were even more prolific than before, now that he was making LPs instead of singles. He kept making up new songs as long as he lived; you could go to one of his shows and hear him sing a blues about a news event that had happened that very day.

Lightnin' Hopkins' success meant recording opportunities for many other Texas rural bluesmen in the postwar years, including two of his cousins. Andrew **"Smokey" Hogg** (1914-1960) made over 100 sides for almost as many labels (it seems), but very few live up to the fine reputation he had as an old-style rural bluesman. Another cousin, **Frankie Lee Sims** (1917-1970), made just a handful of records, but his mix of Texas down-home feel and electric energy is captivating. He's a bit like Lightnin' in overdrive.

The most popular postwar Texas country bluesman next to Lightnin' was Melvin **"Lil'**

FRANKIE LEE SIMS

LUCY MAE BLUES

(Specialty 7022)

Son" Jackson (1916-1976). His 1950 Imperial disc called "Rockin' and Rollin'" was the first recording of the now very familiar blues beginning "Rock me baby, rock me all night long." As a guitarist he played regular patterns with a solid beat, more like Big Bill or Memphis Minnie than like Lightnin''s meanderings. As a singer he had an appealing air of shyness.

Lone Star Guitar Gods

The nationwide 1950s trend toward the B.B. King model for blues—gospel-tinged singing with stinging single-string lead guitar, with West Coast–style horns-and-rhythm backgrounds—found a home in Texas as well, producing some of the hottest guitar-slingers blues has ever known.

LIL' SON JACKSON

TEXAS BLUES

(Arhoolie 352)

His first recordings; track for track, they're his best. The CD also has nice work by several lesser known Texas singers of the period, including Lightnin' Hopkins' old partner Thunder Smith.

THE COMPLETE IMPERIAL RECORDINGS

(Capitol 31744)

You may never get around to hearing all 55 songs, but the best ones are tasty.

BIG MAMA

Willie Mae **"Big Mama" Thornton** (1926-1984) is in the history books as the singer who had a Number One R&B hit with "Hound Dog" three years before Elvis got hold of it, and as composer of the Janis Joplin showstopper "Ball and Chain." Born in Alabama, she spent most of the 1940s touring with a Georgia-based "Hot Harlem Revue" before settling down in Houston where she began recording for the local Peacock label in 1951. Despite the great success of "Hound Dog" she seemed miscast as an R&B singer, unable to find inspiration in the tepid novelty songs and 1940s-style jump blues Peacock asked her to record. Only after she moved to the San Francisco Bay Area in 1957 did she find her true calling, singing a more traditional brand of blues for jazz fans, and for blues revival fans when that began happening in the 1960s. In her prime she was a knockout performer who could remind audiences of Memphis Minnie or even Bessie Smith with her commanding vocals, and also play the drums or take a down-and-dirty harmonica solo. Her later albums give us a snapshot of what she could do.

**BIG MAMA THORNTON
HOUND DOG—THE
PEACOCK RECORDINGS**

(MCA 10668)

BALL AND CHAIN

(Arhoolie 1032)

**GUITAR SLIM:
SUFFERIN' MIND**

(Specialty SPCD 7007)

The First Modern Guitar Heroes?

Nobody in Chicago or anywhere else cranked up his guitar any higher than **Eddie "Guitar Slim" Jones** (1926-1959). The guitar was a weapon for this wild man of the blues, who's credited with being the first to storm through the audience while playing his deafening solos, trailing a 200-foot guitar cord. (Thanks to cordless technology, that's easy nowa-

days.) He made two great records, both recorded on October 27, 1953 in New Orleans with Ray Charles on piano. "The Things That I Used To Do" was the best-selling R&B record of 1954; "The Story Of My Life" has a machine-gun guitar solo that was a primal boyhood inspiration for Frank Zappa's guitar playing. (Jimi Hendrix also cited Slim as an influence.) Pedestrian arrangements drag down many of Slim's other sides, though we can still enjoy his fine lyrics, gospel-tinged singing, and now and then another blast of guitar fire. Slim lived fast, loved hard, and died young at 32.

Johnny "Guitar" Watson (1935-1997) grew up in Texas, moved to Los Angeles at age 15, and soon was fronting his own band, developing an act much like Guitar Slim's. He made one great record, a cover of Earl King's New Orleans hit "Those Lonely, Lonely Nights" with a guitar solo that made a statement: it consisted mostly of one very loud repeated note. Watson also wrote and sang "Gangster of Love," covered by rocker Steve Miller. After fading from sight in the 1960s, Watson successfully reinvented himself as a dance/funk artist in the late 1970s.

BLUES vs. SOUL?

When "soul music" became popular in the 1960s it was often seen as the successor to blues. Indeed, it did steal away a big chunk of blues' original African-American audience. Soul was the new sound; blues was the old, tainted for many young blacks by its association with rural squalor, and by the simple fact that blues was what their parents loved. B.B. King felt the bitter sting of that generation gap when a young audience waiting to hear Sam Cooke and Jackie Wilson booed him when he was introduced as "the blues singer B.B. King."

But is soul music really that different from blues? Yes, and no. Soul music avoids the 12-bar blues chorus like the plague, with its standard harmonic pattern and its statement-and-response lyric plan. Soul composers prefer the harmonic patterns of gospel and pop music. Harmonicas and slide guitars are very scarce in soul music, and so is the century-old wellspring of blues poetry that still flavors blues lyrics. Soul music also arrived with a different rhythmic feel, keyed to the new dance steps of the 1960s.

With singing styles it's harder to draw the line. Soul singing is directly tied to gospel. Blues singers, though, had been drawing more and more on their gospel roots ever since B.B. King rang the wakeup bell with "3 O'Clock Blues" in 1951. Bobby Bland made a seamless transition from blues to soul at the end of the decade (and has continued to blend them seamlessly ever since). The horn sections that are ubiquitous in 1960s soul are a carryover from 1940s and 1950s blues (and, of course, jazz).

Since the early 1980s the line between blues and soul has been straddled if not obliterated by the lively "soul blues" genre; see the "Blues Revival" chapter.

Number One with A Bullet (really)

LITTLE JUNIOR PARKER: THE DUKE RECORDINGS (Volume One)
(MCAD 10669)

Don Robey was one of the most successful and colorful of the many independent record entrepreneurs of the 1940s and 1950s. Like the Chess Brothers in Chicago, he got into the nightclub business first, with a Houston hot spot called the Bronze Peacock. When one of his top draws, Gatemouth Brown, got what he considered shabby treatment from a record company, Robey started Peacock Records, which soon featured such artists as Big Mama Thornton, Johnny Otis and a not-yet-famous Little Richard plus several top gospel groups. His greatest success came after he acquired Memphis-based Duke Records and moved it to Houston. With Duke came the services of Johnny Ace, Little Junior Parker and Bobby Bland, all top 1950s hit-makers. Johnny Ace, who sang mostly ballads, was Duke's first success, selling even more records after he lost a little game of Russian roulette backstage at the Houston City Auditorium on Christmas night, 1954. Bland and Parker survived to make lots more hits with Robey's lo-fi but hip Houston sound.

You hear a lot of stories about those independent R&B label owners...chiseling artists in every way possible, like inventing a fictitious songwriter who claimed half the composer royalties (if not more) on every song the company recorded (the checks went straight to the owner's pocket)...and settling contract disputes at gunpoint. With Don Robey, all that was apparently true. Look for the name "Deadric Malone" on Duke record labels; that was Mr. Robey's phantom songwriter.

CLARENCE GATEMOUTH BROWN

THE ORIGINAL PEACOCK RECORDINGS

(Rounder 2039)

ALRIGHT AGAIN!

(Rounder 2028)
A 1982 Grammy winner.

STANDING MY GROUND

(Alligator AL 4779)
Gatemouth the versatile virtuoso.

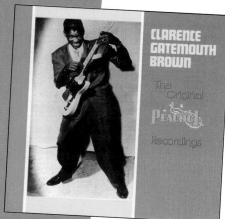

Clarence "Gatemouth" Brown (1924-) was born in Louisiana and grew up in Orange, Texas, much inspired by T-Bone Walker. He also developed quite a taste for country music early on. After wartime Army service he began singing and playing guitar in clubs around Houston, where club-owner Don Robey signed him for his new Peacock record label (see p. 148).

Gatemouth didn't sell tons of records on Peacock, but he laid down some impressive blues over the next decade, including the hottest Texas guitar instrumental of the early 1950s, "Okie Dokie Stomp." He also demonstrated his talents on harmonica and violin. He was just starting to branch out: he moved to Nashville in the 1960s and tried a little country music. Europe in the 1970s was a better bet; the rejuvenated Gatemouth soon re-established himself back home as well, enjoying more success and generally making even better music than he had in the 1950s. Still an ace guitarist, he's become blues' foremost living fiddler. No other bluesman stirs other flavors into his blues quite like Gatemouth.

Freddie King (Freddie Christian, 1934-1976; his first name was often spelled "Freddy") was King of the Blues Instrumentals—"Hide Away," "San-Ho-Zay," "The Stumble," "Sen-Sa-Shun" and dozens more. They dazzled young guitarists (even when they bore names like "Bossa Nova Watusi Twist") and were often covered by white bands in both America and England.

Freddie was born and raised in Texas and based there for much of his career, but he got a lot of his musical education in Chicago where he lived in his twenties and made his first records. There was a lot of both Texas and Chicago in him; his music was a shade more relaxed than that of the Chicago West Side players of his generation, like Buddy Guy, but just as energetic. He was a fine singer ("I'm Tore Down" became a standard), but it was those three-minute instrumental 45s that made him famous. No one could top Freddie at thinking up catchy, memorable guitar riffs and driving them home. One more

thing—those instrumentals were terrific for dancing, at a time when blues was losing sight of that.

He recorded for King Records' Federal label, which went after white buyers with an LP called *Freddie King Goes Surfin'*—a dozen of Freddie's finest with surf sound effects added. After changing labels in 1968, he made several more sophisticated LPs with the rock audience in mind before his death at 42 from heart disease and hepatitis.

FREDDIE KING

HIDE AWAY—THE BEST OF FREDDIE KING
(Rhino 71510)

Albert Collins (1932-1993) was the Ice Man—his high notes sent shivers up your spine. He grew up in Houston listening to T-Bone Walker and Guitar Slim, whose trick of playing guitar from out in the audience he made good use of. Like Freddie King, he made his initial reputation with instrumental 45s. Albert's titles mostly had something to do with ice—"The Freeze," "Frosty," "Sno-Cone," "Frost-Bite," etc. They didn't sell quite like Freddie's did, but they bowled over blues hounds like Canned Heat's Bob "The Bear" Hite, who helped Albert get a record deal with Imperial in 1967. The Imperial LPs made him a national name, and he toured regularly from that point on.

We hadn't seen nothin' yet, as it turned out. He signed with Alligator Records in 1977, and quickly proved to be better than ever. His seven Alligator albums go from strength to strength, proving that Collins wasn't at all the one-trick pony he'd once seemed to be (and doing a lot to establish Alligator as the leading contemporary blues specialist label). The 1985 *Showdown* album featuring Collins along with Johnny Copeland and Robert Cray was a milestone in the modern-day blues revival. He was at the very peak of the profession when he died in 1993.

ALBERT COLLINS

ICE PICKIN'

(Alligator 4713)

LIVE IN JAPAN

(Alligator 4733)

ALBERT COLLINS, ROBERT CRAY, JOHNNY COPELAND: SHOWDOWN!

(Alligator 4743)

Memphis

B.B. King was by no means the only bluesman to make it big in the 1950s by way of Memphis. **(Little) Junior Parker** (Herman Parker, 1932-1971) was a major attraction in the mid-to-late 1950s with hits like "Next Time You See Me" and "Driving Wheel." He also had a connection with that other Memphis hero, Elvis Presley.

He grew up as a singer and harmonica player in the rural tradition, working with both Sonny Boy Williamson #2 and Howlin' Wolf, but only occasionally played harmonica on record. Like Elvis he recorded for Sun, scoring his first hit with a John Lee Hooker-inspired boogie called "Feelin' Good" and following that up with his original "Mystery Train," which Elvis turned into his finest blues record.

Parker was soon hired away by Duke Records, which had recently been taken over by Houston record mogul Don Robey and moved to that city. Parker moved there too and gradually became one of Duke's top artists. Though his first Duke releases resembled the Sun sides, Duke gradually shifted him to horns-and-rhythm settings which nicely suited his rather sweet voice with its pronounced vibrato. Since Parker didn't play guitar, Duke brought in Pat Hare, who later joined the Muddy Waters band (and still later was sent to prison for life after murdering his girlfriend and a cop). Parker recorded for Duke and played the chitlin' circuit until the mid-1960s; his death of a brain tumor at age 39 robbed him of a chance to reach revival audiences.

Parker's labelmate **Bobby "Blue" Bland** (1930-) was Duke's biggest hitmaker: "Farther Up The Road," "I Pity The Fool," "Turn On Your Love Light" and "That's The Way Love Is" are just a few of his best-sellers for the label in the 1950s and early 1960s, all blessed with the fine arrangements of Duke's house bandleader Joe Scott and the playing of guitarist Wayne Bennett (Bland normally doesn't play an instrument).

From 1960 onward Bland sang mostly soul music, which was rapidly replacing blues in the affections of younger black listeners. The difference didn't seem to matter as much to him as it did to blues historians. Eventually it didn't matter much to anyone, as blues and soul grew closer together in the 1980s and 1990s (See "Blues vs. Soul?"). Bobby Bland remains a favorite today, bridging most of what few gaps there are between segments of the greater blues community.

BOBBY BLAND

THE BEST OF BOBBY BLAND

(MCA 31219)

"The Best of Bobby Bland"

Poverty ·
I Smell Trouble ·
Some-day ·
I'll Take Care Of You ·
I Pity The Fool ·
Cry Cry Cry ·
Turn On Your Love Light ·
Call On Me ·
Stormy Monday ·
Ain't Nothing You Can Do ·
Farther Up The Road ·
IF YOU COULD READ
MY MIND

One of the greatest blues discoveries of the 1960s was a man who never showed much Gospel influence at all but still had a strong soul music connection. **Albert King** (1923-1992) was born in Indianola, Miss., (later to be B.B. King's home, but the two aren't related). He made the standard Mississippi-Chicago trek in the early 1950s, played drums behind Jimmy Reed for a while, and made a solitary record before leaving for greener pastures in St. Louis. There, he became a local favorite and recorded one fair-sized national R&B hit ("Don't Throw Your Love On Me So Strong," 1961) but couldn't follow that up with anything comparable...until a Memphis record company which had recorded some of the nation's biggest soul music hits decided to take a chance with him.

There'd never been anything quite like Albert King's records for Stax. Produced by the same team that made the hits for Otis Redding, Sam & Dave and Rufus Thomas, backed by the same rhythm section (a.k.a.

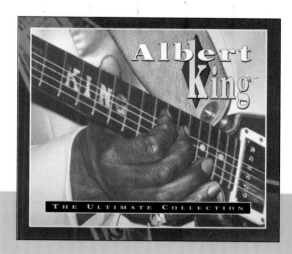

ALBERT KING

THE ULTIMATE COLLECTION

(Rhino 71268)

It's all here on these 2 CDs, from that first Chicago session through his St. Louis period, the great Stax hits and what came after.

Booker T. & the M.G.'s), they stripped Albert's blues down to the nitty gritty, and gave it a rhythmic feel that beggared numerous other contemporary attempts to match blues to 1960s dance steps. There was plenty of space for the unique sound of Albert's guitar—which is unique partly because he played left-handed, without reversing the normal order of the strings as most left-handed players do. Like B.B. he didn't use a slide but had his own distinctive way of bending the notes—as recognizably different from B. B.'s as his signature (which it was).

Albert not only reconnected with the black blues audience but reached out to the young white audience as well. At the grand opening of San Francisco's Fillmore West, he shared a bill with Jimi Hendrix and John Mayall.

All good things must come to an end, including the Stax studios. Though King never again made records quite so fine, he made lots of good ones, and remained a great concert performer until a heart attack felled him at 69.

New Orleans

New Orleans is the home of an instantly recognizable brand of buoyant, infectious R&B, known for its sunny major-key melodies, lively piano accompaniment and its syncopated rhythms—kin to the fabled "second lines" of the city's jazz tradition, and a reminder of the port city's links to Latin America and Africa.

We don't know exactly how that music got started. Not much blues was recorded in New Orleans until 1948, when entrepreneur-engineer Cosimo Matassa set up a tiny studio that soon began turning out R&B hits like Roy Brown's "Good Rockin' Tonight," Fats Domino's "The Fat Man" and Lloyd Price's "Lawdy Miss Clawdy." The "New Orleans sound" stayed hot through the 1960s, contributing as much to rock 'n' roll and soul music as it did to blues…but blues was where it started.

Singer-pianist **Professor Longhair** (Henry Roeland "Roy" Byrd, 1918-1980) is often called the founding father of New Orleans R&B. For most of his career "Fess" barely made a living from his music, but in the last decade of his life he was discovered by the blues revival audience and revered as a living legend at the annual New Orleans Jazz and Heritage Festival and around the world. The city's most famous blues nightclub, Tipitina's, is named after one of Fess' songs.

A street hustler and professional gambler, Fess became a professional entertainer after World War II. In 1949 his band Professor Longhair and his Shuffling Hungarians recorded "She Ain't Got No Hair" for a tiny Texas label. That was enough of a local hit to interest Mercury Records, which re-recorded the song under the name "Bald Head." It came out under the name Roy Byrd and his Blues Jumpers (thereby placating the company's Hungarian customers, we presume) and provided Fess with his one and only national hit in 1950.

Fess recorded for numerous labels in the 1950s, including "Tipitina" for Atlantic in 1954 and "Go To The Mardi Gras" in 1959 for Ronn, one of the city's first hometown record labels. That song has been a Mardi Gras anthem ever since, but none of those records were heard much outside New Orleans until they were reissued in the 1970s. The '70s were not a great decade for blues, but thankfully Fess was able to enjoy a few rewards for a life of great music.

The man who put New Orleans R&B on the map was Antoine **"Fats" Domino** (1928-). At age 21, his first release "The Fat Man" led off a hit parade that didn't let up until well into the 1960s, mostly on the L.A.-based Imperial label. (New Orleans didn't have any significant R&B labels of its own until 1958.) When the rock 'n' roll boom arrived, he was one of the first African-American artists to cross over to the pop charts. Oldies fans may remember him as the friendly face behind rocking revivals of ancient pop songs like "Blueberry Hill" and "My Blue Heaven," but for his first five years of fame Fats was strictly a bluesman, and a fine one.

His urban piano blues was a direct descendant of Leroy Carr's, but it sounded fresh and new in 1950. One reason is that New Orleans major-key thing. Even "Goin' To The River," a song about jumping off a bridge, somehow seems warm and comforting with that pretty, sing-along melody. Fats' lyrics and melodies are simple, direct and appealing. As with Jimmy Reed, his records could be rather similar to each other, but people kept coming back for more. Though Fats doesn't use syncopation as much as other New Orleans artists, it does sneak in now and then.

PROFESSOR LONGHAIR

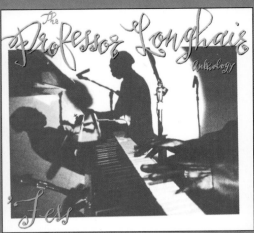

CRAWFISH FIESTA

(Alligator 4718)

Released on the very day he died. Fess was still making terrific music.

'FESS: THE PROFESSOR LONGHAIR ANTHOLOGY

(Rhino 71502)

A 2-CD career retrospective.

Again as with Reed, Fats' songs and records were collaborations. **Dave Bartholomew** (1920-) wrote a great many of the songs and produced the records. He did the same for other artists as well, in addition to making a good many records himself as a singer and bandleader. His role in shaping the New Orleans R&B sound was a bit like Willie Dixon's in Chicago.

Though Bartholomew produced most of his hits for Imperial Records, he moonlighted a little. For another L.A. company, Specialty, he produced "Lawdy Miss Clawdy" by **Lloyd Price** (1932-) with Fats Domino on piano. Price's passionate pleading was quite a contrast to Fats' own serene singing. It was the biggest R&B record hit of 1952, a big feather in the cap of the New Orleans scene. Price would soon move away from blues to the pop-soul style heard on late-1950s hits like "Stagger Lee" and "Personality."

Back at Imperial, Bartholomew recorded **Smiley Lewis** (Overton Lemons, 1920-1966) for seven years. There were a couple of good-sized hits: "The Bells Are Ringing" (1952, with a melody almost identical to that of "Lawdy Miss Clawdy") and "I Hear You

FATS DOMINO

THE EARLY IMPERIAL SINGLES

(Ace [UK] 597)

Knocking" (1955, a song covered by pop singer Gale Storm that year, and by Dave Edmunds in 1970, both Top Five pop hits). Lewis, who didn't play an instrument, sounds a bit like a blues shouter in the Joe Turner mode; the menace in his voice on "Knocking" makes a nice contrast with those sunny major chords behind him. Another song of his, "One Night," was covered by Elvis Presley, who toned down the lyrics a bit ("One night of sin" became "One night with you").

New Orleans blues in the 1950s wasn't noted for lead guitarists, but it had a good one in **Earl King** (Solomon Johnson, 1934-) who played on numerous local recording sessions, wrote a stack of fine songs, and had a few hits himself including the much-imitated blues ballad "Those Lonely, Lonely Nights" (1955). He returned to performing and recording in the 1980s.

What Dave Bartholomew was to the 1950s, **Allen Toussaint** (1938-) has been to the 1960s and more recent decades. A producer, songwriter, pianist and occasional singer, Toussaint creates records whose subtle (or sometimes obvious) use of those New Orleans syncopations makes you move your body, whatever the musical style. (He's done everything from gutbucket blues to mellow singer-songwriters). He had an especially hot run of hits in 1961 with "Mother-In-Law" by Ernie K-Doe, "I Like It Like That" by Chris Kenner and "Ya Ya" by Lee Dorsey. Five years later, his production of Dorsey's "Get Out Of My Life, Woman" turned heads everywhere with its sledgehammer backbeat and shining simplicity. (Toussaint also wrote the bluesy song.)

The annals of New Orleans are packed with great R&B singers and musicians whose music mixes blues elements with rock 'n' roll and soul: Huey Smith, Clarence "Frog Man" Henry, Paul Gayten, James "Sugar Boy" Crawford, Jessie Hill, Robert Parker. New Orleans R&B sometimes seems like one big happy family. If you get the impression that every New Orleans bluesman has at one time or another worked with every other New Orleans bluesman, you're not far off the mark. Of course there've been unhappy stories too…keyboard player **James Booker** (1939-1983) was one of the busiest and most talented musicians in town until his career was derailed by drugs and mental illness. At 21 he had a national hit single with the organ instrumental "Gonzo," a cheerful dance piece that presaged the Memphis music of Booker T. & the M.G.'s. A pair of Rounder albums preserve the eccentric but brilliant music he made on occasion in his later years.

We'll conclude with the happier story of **Mac Rebbennack** (1940-), the multi-instrumental whiz who played guitar, bass and piano on countless local record sessions before he was 20, and re-invented himself in the 1960s as the psychedelic voodoo shaman Dr. John the Night Tripper. Nowadays he's called simply Dr. John; he sings and plays an awesome variety of music, from Tin Pan Alley classics to vintage New Orleans blues. No two Dr. John albums are alike. Meanwhile, the Neville Brothers, who have performed and recorded under various names since the 1950s, continue to breathe life into a wealth of timeless New Orleans music.

"Swamp Blues" in Baton Rouge

Seventy-five miles west of New Orleans, the state capital of Baton Rouge hosted a very different local blues scene in the postwar years, with a more rural flavor. It featured electric guitars and harmonicas like Chicago, but the laid-back feel was more like Texas.

Another 75 miles west, out in Cajun country, an electrical contractor named Jay Miller opened a recording studio in the town of Crowley. He started out with Cajun and country music, but in 1954 became interested in a Baton Rouge blues singer called Lightnin' Slim. After a few Lightnin' Slim records on his own Feature label became local hits, Miller cut a deal with a Nashville label called Excello Records for national distribution. For the next decade a steady stream of Crowley-recorded Baton Rouge blues appeared on Excello 45s. They bucked the prevailing 1950s–early 1960s trend—no gospel-y singing here, no screaming guitar leads, no horns. In spite of that (or because of that) they appealed to a faithful clientele and occasionally reached the national charts. Blues connoisseurs around the world sought out and treasured those singles, nicknaming them "swamp blues."

Lightnin' Slim (Otis Hicks, 1913-1974) was the dean of the scene—born two years before Muddy Waters. He began playing at Louisiana country gatherings in the 1930s but didn't become a pro until moving to Baton Rouge after World War II. History doesn't tell us how he got his nickname, but Lightnin' Hopkins definitely had fans in the area. Slim's voice was darker and rougher, though. His blues had a ponderous, deliberate quality which could be very moving, but definitely wasn't hip in the 1950s. (Slim's original fans were not looking for hip.) Eventually he moved to Detroit and drifted out of music, though he managed a brief comeback (mostly in Europe) before dying of cancer at 61.

The fastest horse in Miller's stable turned out to

be **Slim Harpo** (James Moore, 1924-1970). He had two big national hits, the blues ballad "Rainin' In My Heart" (1961) and the sly, sexy dance novelty "Baby Scratch My Back" (1966). He also wrote and originally recorded "I'm A King Bee," covered by the Rolling Stones, and "Got Love If You Want It," covered by the Kinks.

Born in Baton Rouge, he'd been singing and playing harmonica all over South Louisiana for well over a decade before Miller found him. He was "Harmonica Slim" until Miller decided a more original name was in order. "Rainin' In My Heart" put Harpo on the chitlin' circuit all over the South. "Baby Scratch My Back" made him a rock star, playing the Fillmore East in New York and the Whiskey-a-Go-Go in Los Angeles as well as NYC's legendary Apollo Theater. He might still be a rock star today if he hadn't died of a heart attack at 46 on a visit back home to Baton Rouge.

The most active survivor of the "swamp blues" scene is **Lazy Lester** (Leslie Johnson, 1933-) who played harmonica on many Lightnin' Slim records and also sang on a few of his own, notably "I'm A Lover, Not A Fighter" and "Sugar Coated Love." Like Light-

nin' Slim, he moved to Michigan and got a day job after the Baton Rouge– Crowley scene tailed off. Twenty years later the blues revival found him alive and well, and he's waved the swamp blues flag ever since on CDs and in person.

One imagines there might have been blues scenes as fertile as Baton Rouge's in small cities all over the South,

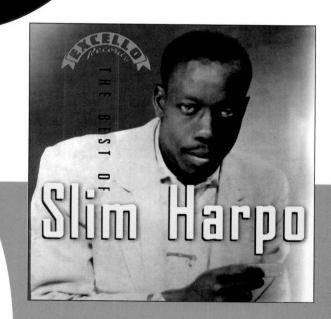

SLIM HARPO

THE BEST OF SLIM HARPO
(MCA/HIP'O 40072)

LAZY LESTER

HARP AND SOUL

(Alligator 4768)

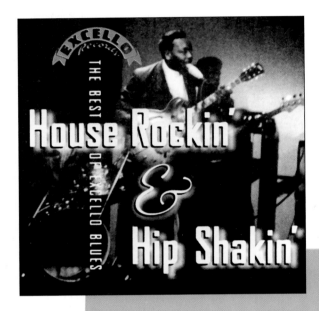

that lacked only a Jay Miller to preserve their music for posterity. Swamp blues is a fertile field today, having evolved into a kind of pan-Louisianan music that brings in elements of country, Cajun and zydeco music and good old rock 'n' roll along with what it started with.

EXCELLO RECORDS

THE BEST OF EXCELLO RECORDS

**HOUSE ROCKIN' & HIP SHAKIN':
The Best Of Excello Blues**

(Hip-O HIPD-40071)
Features the Baton Rouge artists named here and several other worthy contenders.

Zydeco

That marvelous mix of Cajun music and R&B called **zydeco** was another great Louisiana invention of the 1950s. It started as a strictly local thing, the homespun music of black share-croppers who lived in Cajun country, and adapted the language and music of the neighborhood.

You can hear zydeco around the world today, which is mostly due to **Clifton Chenier** (1925-1987). Clifton was to zydeco what Bob Marley was to reggae, a terrific performer and showman who was also a great ambassador for the music. He grew up and learned to play accordion the old way on a farm near Opelousas, La., but also heard plenty of current R&B on the radio. He and his brother Cleveland (who played washboard) worked a while with Clarence Garlow, whose jump blues with bilingual lyrics helped pave the way for zydeco.

(He had a national R&B hit with "Bon Ton Roula" in 1950.) Then the Cheniers formed their own band, playing what was essentially R&B with accordion lead and occasional French vocals. They recorded here and there, attracting some attention with their Specialty single "Ay-Tete-Fee" (the record company's phonetic approximation of "Ay, Petite Fille" i.e. "Hey, Little Girl"). Chenier's career didn't really blossom until Arhoolie Records, Chris Strachwitz's Berkeley-based label which had recorded several Texas bluesmen for the folk audience, signed Chenier and encouraged him to ditch the generic R&B and play rootsier music. The

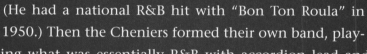

**CLIFTON CHENIER
BOGALUSA BOOGIE**

(Arhoolie 347)

**LOUISIANA BLUES
AND ZYDECO**

(Arhoolie 329)

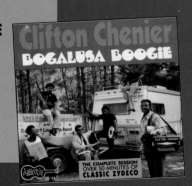

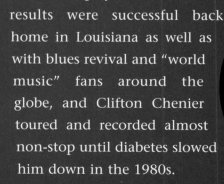

results were successful back home in Louisiana as well as with blues revival and "world music" fans around the globe, and Clifton Chenier toured and recorded almost non-stop until diabetes slowed him down in the 1980s.

PART FOUR

THE REVIVAL BLUES

Chapter 9

The Acoustic and Electric Rebirths

Many of our little biographical sketches in the last few chapters have included words to the effect that "the hits stopped coming in the 1960s" or "audiences declined in the 1960s." It was part demographics—people who had supported blues since the 1940s or earlier were reaching an age where they didn't go to a nightclub or buy records as often as before. It also had to do with the natural change of fashions—in with the new, out with the old. Few young people anywhere are fans of their parents' favorite music.

And so in African America, blues was getting to be old hat in the 1960s. Fortunately, that was also a decade when many young white Americans became avid blues fans. It was all new to them, exotic yet fulfilling, novel yet ageless.

The "blues revival" was really a series of several blues revivals. In stage one (early 1960s), white devotees of traditional folk music and its variations discovered black acoustic blues. In stage two (mid- to late 1960s), young white musicians and their white fans discovered black electric blues.

BROWNIE McGHEE & SONNY TERRY at the 2nd Fret

This happened separately in England and in America. Then there was a period of decline (the 1970s) before stage three (starting around 1980) in which blues grew into the phenomenon it is today.

Stage One: Acoustic

The roots of the acoustic stage of the blues revival go back before World War II…to 1935, when Lead Belly settled in New York City after having been discovered in a Louisiana prison by John and Alan Lomax. Josh White arrived from South Carolina around the same time, and both artists began entertaining a small but influential audience of left-leaning intellectuals, and making a few records for that audience.

After World War II that audience grew, as did the audience for folk music in general—Burl Ives, Pete Seeger and The Weavers. In the 1950s, White became a major attraction at nightclubs all over the country and abroad. He expertly tailored his music for the white audience of the day, and it had little to do with the blues that black audiences were enjoying at that time, but at least some of it was blues. Meanwhile, the team of **Brownie McGhee** (1915-1996) and **Sonny Terry** (1911-1986) became very popular. Both had worked with Blind Boy Fuller in North Carolina before his death

in 1940. After that they moved to New York, where they appeared separately and together in nightclubs and concerts; Terry was in the Broadway musical *Finian's Rainbow*. They also continued to make 78s and 45s for the black audience until the late 1950s. For white audiences they sang the same easygoing Piedmont-style blues they'd known since the 1930s, interspersed with old folksongs such as "John Henry" and Sonny's harmonica showpieces like "Fox Chase."

Another great Piedmont guitarist—who actually taught Blind Boy Fuller some of his tricks—**Rev. Gary Davis** (1899-1972) began working the New York folk audience in the late 1940s, giving guitar lessons on the side. By the 1960s he was drawing crowds across the country in the same nightclubs and coffeehouses where McGhee and Terry played.

Meanwhile **Jesse Fuller** (1896-1976) toured the circuit from his home base in Oakland, Ca., doing his one-man-band act with twelve-string guitar and "fotdella" (a home-made bass played with pedals) and singing blues and folksongs he remembered from his youth in Georgia plus his popular original "San Francisco Bay Blues."

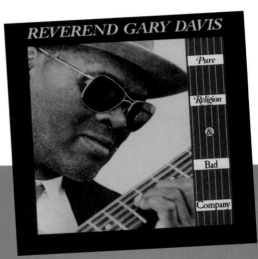

BROWNIE
McGHEE
&
SONNY
TERRY

MR. BROWNIE AND MR. SONNY

(Prestige 9913)

REV.
GARY
DAVIS

PURE RELIGION AND BAD COMPANY

(Smithsonian-Folkways 40035)

MANCE LIPSCOMB

TEXAS SONGSTER

(Arhoolie 306)

**TEXAS SONGSTER VOL. 2
(YOU GOT TO REAP WHAT YOU SOW)**

(Arhoolie 398)

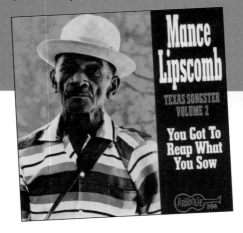

Among the first of these was **Mance Lipscomb** (1895-1976), a songster from Navasota, Texas, with a boundless repertoire and an engaging style. He was one of those untold thousands of fine singers the pre-war record companies never got to. He'd just been minding his business in Navasota, playing for decades of parties and picnics where he had to fill requests for everything from the latest blues hits to "It Ain't Gonna Rain No Mo'" and "Shine On Harvest Moon." His music, rather like Mississippi John Hurt's but with a stronger beat for the dancers, enraptured folk revival audiences much as John's did…leaving Mance a bit perplexed at first. "I wonder if the people are having a good time," he said once after a young audience at the Ash Grove coffeehouse in

In the 1960s—as the folk revival became a mass movement thanks to The Kingston Trio, Joan Baez, Peter, Paul & Mary, Bob Dylan, etc. etc.—these worthies were joined on the coffeehouse and concert circuits by a number of great bluesmen and songsters who had recorded in the pre-WWII days and had just been "rediscovered": Mississippi John Hurt, Bukka White, Sleepy John Estes, Son House, Skip James. Just as importantly, artists of the same generations who had not previously made a name for themselves on records shared their music with adoring young audiences.

Original LP graphics for the CDs now in print.

Los Angeles had respectfully enjoyed an hour of his music. "They're so quiet…they don't make noise while I'm playing like the folks do down home." His first album was also the first album for Arhoolie Records, a Northern California–based label that has since recorded dozens of other songsters and bluesmen along with a great deal of ethnic music from other cultures. Lipscomb's art was also well documented on film before he died at 80.

Another great discovery was Mississippi bluesman **Fred McDowell** (1904-1972). Alan Lomax found him in 1959, running a scraggly little farm in the hills just east of the Delta, and playing and singing Delta-style blues as if it were 1929. Though his music had all the hallmarks of the Delta, it didn't obviously resemble Charlie Patton or any other known Delta stylist, and indeed McDowell had little contact with any of the area's recording artists during the heyday of Delta blues.

Songs of his like "Write Me A Few Lines" might have made popular and influential records back then. Instead, his music cast its spell on another generation. In 1963 he hit the revival circuit and was soon counted among the greatest living bluesmen. The Rolling Stones recorded his "You Gotta Move." Bonnie Raitt credited him with inspiring her

slide guitar style. He appeared in several documentary films, and toured frequently until shortly before his death.

Robert Pete Williams (1914-1981) was even more of an individualist. He was inspired as a young man by Blind Lemon Jefferson records, and he shares Lemon's free timing and fast fretwork. But there the resemblance ends. Whereas Lemon was the great entertainer, Robert Pete played mostly for his own catharsis. In 1956 he killed a man in a barroom brawl (he insisted it was self defense) and was sentenced to Angola State Prison Farm in Louisiana, where folklorist Harry Oster found and recorded him three years later (and secured his parole, as John Lomax had done with Leadbelly at the same institution in 1934).

While Williams' blues may have been too dark, grim and foreboding to make him a popular performer in his Louisiana hometown, the revival audience was looking for seriousness and depth. Williams gave it to them, along with his unique guitar playing, and was able to make a decent living for the first time in his life.

David (Honeyboy) Edwards (1915-) is a Delta bluesman who as a young man sang and played with all the legends—Robert Johnson, Big Joe Williams, Tommy McClennan,

FRED McDOWELL

YOU GOTTA MOVE

(Arhoolie 304)

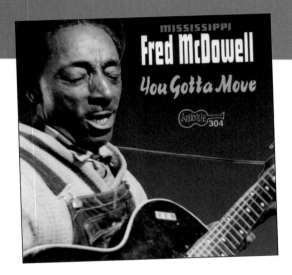

even Charlie Patton. He recorded for one of Alan Lomax's Library of Congress expeditions in 1942, and did a little performing and recording in Chicago in the 1950s, but his career didn't blossom until historians introduced him to the revival audience in the mid-1960s. He has played many a festival since then, promoted as one of the last survivors of a golden era of blues, sounding very good considering all that.

◆

With pre-WWII acoustic blues getting all that welcome exposure in the 1960s, young white singers and guitarists naturally sought to make it their own, just as young Southern whites like Jimmie Rodgers had back in the 1920s. One of them had impeccable credentials: **John Hammond** (Jr.) (1942-), son of the record producer and promoter who had recorded Bessie Smith and Billie Holiday, and promoted that 1938 Carnegie Hall concert where he wanted Robert Johnson but settled for Big Bill Broonzy. John Jr. picked the very best songs from Dad's record collection (with Johnson of course a special favorite), played them quite impeccably on guitar, and sang them strongly if occasionally overdramatically.

That, plus his movie star looks, made him rather popular. He never quite became a superstar, but three-plus decades later he's still doing it. His music is a bit leaner and

ROBERT PETE WILLIAMS

FREE AGAIN

(Original Blues Classics OBC-553)

tougher now, sounding better than ever really, and he's still looking good too.

Out in Minneapolis, **Koerner, Ray and Glover** worked similar musical territory with a bit more originality, looking the part in their scruffy jeans. The trio wrote quite a bit of its own material, and had a distinctive style that didn't owe too much to any particular black artist. They still draw a crowd in the Twin Cities for their occasional shows, together and separately. Tony Glover wrote a popular blues harmonica instruction book.

Rory Block (1949-) learned her acoustic blues in the 1960s, but her career didn't blossom until much more recently. She grew up in New York's Greenwich Village where her father's sandal shop was a folk musicians' hangout. As a teenager she saw and learned from all the "rediscoveries" who came to perform in Manhattan, and got to know many of them. However, by the time she grew up, the acoustic blues revival was pretty much history. She attempted a career as a pop singer with little success. In 1989, though, she signed with folk label Rounder Records. Her first CD, *High Heeled Blues*, was actually a more convincing take on pre-WWII acoustic blues than any white singer had managed in the 1960s. It sold well, and Block has continued to record regularly ever

BLUES, RAGS AND HOLLERS

"SPIDER" JOHN KOERNER, DAVE "SNAKER" RAY
AND TONY "LITTLE SUN" GLOVER

since, mixing the works of Robert Johnson, Skip James, etc. with her fine originals. Though her strong and straightforward singing style is her own, the acoustic guitar riffs and patterns are perfect pre-war Delta.

Stage Two: British Electric

While Americans were singing along with Pete Seeger or sighing to Joan Baez, the British were skiffling. Skiffle music was ostensibly inspired by American jug and washboard bands of the 1920s. It didn't really sound much like those, but skifflers did sing Leadbelly songs and other blues-like material, and the guitar was often bluesy and sometimes electrified. (American folkies shunned amplifiers in those days.) The Beatles, as everyone knows, began as a skiffle group and made an easy transition to rock 'n' roll.

So it shouldn't be a surprise that Britain, not the U.S.A., had the first notable white electric blues band. **Blues Incorporated**, founded in 1961 by guitarist Alexis Korner and singer/harmonica player Cyril Davies, both of whom had played in various jazz and skiffle groups. Charlie Watts, later of the Rolling Stones, was the original drummer. Personnel changed frequently and guest musicians were welcomed.

RORY BLOCK

HIGH HEELED BLUES

(Rounder 3061)

AIN'T I A WOMAN

(Rounder 3120)

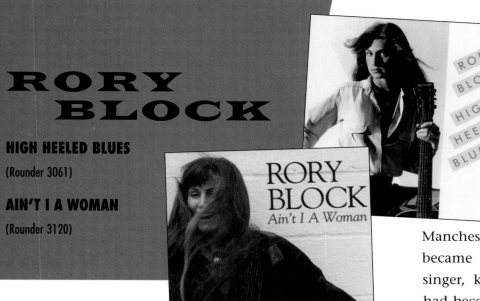

Though the band never had a hit record, its London performances were magnets for young musicians including Mick Jagger, Keith Richards and Brian Jones, who formed their own band after meeting at a Blues Incorporated jam session.

That band was of course **The Rolling Stones,** named after a track on an American import album in Brian's collection, *The Best Of Muddy Waters*. The early Stones were a blues band all the way, complete with harmonica. Their first album had covers of songs by Willie Dixon, Jimmy Reed, Bo Diddley and Slim Harpo, along with Chuck Berry and Rufus

Thomas. The only thing missing was the reverence!

Though the Stones soon went in a different direction, they've paid lip service and sometimes quite a bit more to blues through the years. Meanwhile **John Mayall** (1933-) moved from Manchester to London in 1963 and soon became Britain's best-known bluesman. A singer, keyboard and harmonica player, he had become familiar with blues via his dad's record collection which included rare imports from America. His band, the Bluesbreakers, had the same sort of revolving-door membership as Blues Incorporated. It became known

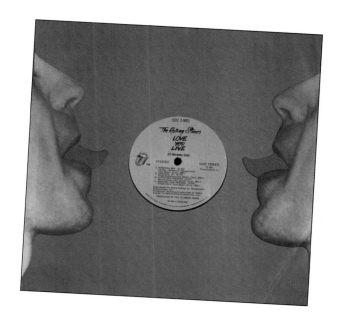

as a sort of school for British blues musicians, especially when it began accompanying visiting American bluesmen for club gigs in England.

One of Mayall's lead guitarists became very well known indeed. **Eric Clapton** (1945-) was already fairly famous when he joined the Bluesbreakers in 1965, having left The Yardbirds when their music became too "pop" for his liking. He only stayed a year with Mayall, but the one album he made with him, *Bluesbreakers–John Mayall with Eric Clapton* (1966) is for many the all-time high-water mark of British blues. At age 21 Clapton astonished listeners with his command of blues lead guitar, particularly the Chicago West Side version *a la* Otis Rush...with frequent reminders of B. B. and of Freddie King, whose "Hideaway" is a highlight of the set. The band's fans (who, it must be noted, were not neccessarily familiar with Otis Rush or Freddie King) decorated the walls of London with the famous graffito "Clapton Is God."

More on Clapton shortly. Two more lead guitarists followed him through the Mayall School of Blues—Peter Green, who made *A Hard Road* with Mayall and left for Fleetwood Mac, and Mick Taylor, who played lead on *Crusade* before replacing the departed Brian Jones in the Stones. Mayall then began explor-

ing other areas of blues—acoustic blues, jazz-blues, soul-blues. He's done that ever since, returning every so often to the hard-driving sounds of the Bluesbreakers days. The Mayall School is still in session.

Some might be surprised to see **Fleetwood Mac** in a blues book...but seven years before Americans Lindsey Buckingham and Stevie Nicks joined the group to make *Rumours*, etc., Fleetwood Mac was a fine British blues band. The original members included three ex-Bluesbreakers—guitarist Peter Green, bassist John McVie and drummer-namesake Mick Fleetwood, plus slide guitar specialist Jeremy Spencer. The first album was almost all hard blues, quite up to Bluesbreaker standards, and a great success in England. The second had the original blues "Black Magic Woman," covered in the U.S.A. by Santana, and the exquisite instrumental "Albatross," a million-seller in the U.K.

JOHN MAYALL

BLUESBREAKERS: JOHN MAYALL WITH ERIC CLAPTON
(London 800 086)

Shortly afterward, Peter Green became convinced that playing lead guitar in a blues-rock band wasn't compatible with his religion. Jeremy Spencer made the same decision (different denomination) in the midst of an American tour. (Green returned to blues in the late 1990s.) Their replacements made excellent music that's outside the scope of this book.

Other notable blues-rock came from outside the Mayall orbit. **The Animals** featured lead singer Eric Burdon, a passionate blues fan. They had a hit with John Lee Hooker's "Boom Boom" and a bigger one with "The House of the Rising Sun," a folksong recorded by both Leadbelly and Josh White, with the Animals' version closer to the latter's. Their bass player, "Chas" Chandler, made his greatest contribution to history after leaving the group. Visiting New York in 1966, he saw a young black guitarist known as Jimmy James in a club there, and talked him into moving to London to form a new group.

Jimmy James soon became much better known as **Jimi Hendrix** (1942-1970), a guitarist who transformed the world of rock and also left a big footprint in blues history in his short career. Just as Muddy Waters had discovered that the sound of amplifier distortion could be desirable and musical, and Little Walter had learned to use the idiosyncracies of a cheap mike to his advantage, Hendrix turned the malfunctions of modern megawatt amplifiers into beautiful music. He taught himself how to hold a gui-

JIMI HENDRIX

BLUES

(MCA need number)

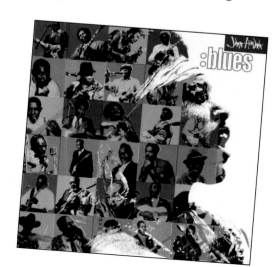

tar so that the sound from the amp would feed back into its pickups just so, making a note as lyrical as a violin's (but a thousand times louder!). He was equally inventive in the recording studio, endlessly experimenting with electronic devices to expand the guitar's sonic versatility.

The notes he played on that guitar were often blues; he learned his first licks from records by B.B. King and Muddy Waters. At 19, he hit the road, and for the next five years paid his dues and honed his licks playing behind every R&B act you could name and many you couldn't, cutting the occasional 45 (including one with Little Richard for Vee-Jay, "I Don't Know What You've Got [But It's Got Me]"). After Chandler put together The Jimi Hendrix Experience with two British musicians, Hendrix toured and recorded for three-plus glorious years before the rock 'n' roll fast life caught up to him. Blues people still play his licks today, or use a bit of feedback to their advantage; his slow blues "Red House" has become a standard.

◆

The Yardbirds, the group Eric Clapton quit because they had become too "pop" for him, had set out in 1964 as dedicated missionaries bent on converting the British Isles to the Chicago electric blues gospel. With Clapton on the

point and the Rolling Stones promoting them, they were soon the talk of London. Their 1964 LP *Five Live Yardbirds* has more nervous energy than real power...but remember, none of them were over 21, and Clapton was just 19.

The group invited Jimmy Page to replace Clapton, and when he declined got Jeff Beck, with whom they made some wondrous psychedelia with an occasional taste of blues. Page eventually got on board as well, and inherited the group's name when it fell apart in 1968. He put together a group called the New Yardbirds, which changed its name to **Led Zeppelin** after recording an album containing two Willie Dixon songs.

A lead zeppelin is a very heavy thing. With the most earth-shaking amplification, the most athletic guitar playing, the loudest and highest singing, Led Zeppelin bludgeoned the competition into submission, not to mention the blues songs they did. It didn't sound much like blues or feel anything like blues...but for a generation of rockers, Led Zeppelin was the most profound music within easy reach. It affected people deeply, and along the way it planted a tiny seed of blues in the subconscious, which perhaps sprouted and grew a few years later when those people heard some real blues in the right setting. And...

when Willie Dixon finally got some royalties for that tune of his that Led Zep borrowed for "Whole Lotta Love," they went a long way toward building the Blues Heaven Foundation.

◆

Now back to Eric Clapton. After leaving John Mayall's Bluesbreakers, he formed Cream with drummer Ginger Baker and fellow ex-Bluesbreaker Jack Bruce on bass. Though Clapton hoped for a hard-core blues band, Cream didn't always work out that way, due to the need to do something commercially successful and his band-mates' preference for jazz. The blues Cream did produce on its second and third LPs was, however, excellent and very successful commercially. On *Disraeli Gears* Clapton got to do a perfect Albert King solo on "Strange Brew," and another blazing solo on the hit "Sunshine Of Your Love" (which is based on an innovative double-length blues chorus). *Wheels of Fire* brought us "Crossroads," Clapton's high-energy rock-out on Robert Johnson's "Cross Road Blues." He sang it decently and played it brilliantly. By traditional blues standards, it might have been a bit frenetic and excessive (the 4 1/2-minute recording was edited down from a much longer live performance) but rock

ERIC CLAPTON

FROM THE CRADLE
(Duck/Reprise 45735)

CROSSROADS
(Polydor 835 261)
A 4-CD career retrospective.

fans loved it. No doubt many of them got curious who the hell this Robert Johnson was, and were thereby drawn deeper into the wondrous mysteries of blues.

Cream went sour soon after that, and it was not a pretty sight. On his own, Clapton began exploring the quieter melodic virtues of other kinds of music, pop, rock, soul and country. (Alas, he also began exploring heroin.) After the short-lived Blind Faith he formed Derek and the Dominoes. The title track of their album *Layla* (featuring a guitar duet with Duane Allman) is one of the best-loved rock classics of the 1970s, but that band lasted no longer than Blind Faith had. Before long, though, Clapton discovered that he could sell a lot of albums as a pop-rock singer, which is essentially what he did for the next 20 years (along with cleaning up his lifestyle). Most albums contained a blues or two, and in concert he was always good for some classy blues guitar work.

In the 1990s Clapton began feeling that he hadn't yet recorded the best blues he was capable of, and also a desire to shine some more light on the music that had always inspired him so. In 1994 he recorded *From the Cradle*, a CD that comes awfully close to perfection as a revival project. All the tracks are covers of blues from the 1960s and earlier, familiar and not so familiar. There are songs by Leroy Carr, Eddie Boyd, Muddy Waters, Jimmy Rogers, Lowell Fulson, Elmore James and Freddie King; the radio hit was a version of Barbecue Bob's 1927 "Motherless Chile Blues." Some are remarkably close to the old records; others are innovative (Charles Brown's "Drifting Blues" is done *a la* John Lee Hooker; "Motherless Child" starts with the original Barbecue Bob sound, then adds a surging rock rhythm section). Clapton's singing is, for a change, very nearly as fine as his playing. The album was as big commercially as anything he had ever done (reaching #1 on the charts) and those millions of buyers got some damn fine blues—a superb introduction to the genre for anyone who needs one.

Stage Two: American Electric

The American white electric blues scene of the 1960s was quite different from the British version, and quite independent of it. It took longer to get started,

Paul Butterfield Blues Band

it never got the attention British blues got, and several key performers were laid low by drugs, but it produced some highly original and excellent blues.

The **Paul Butterfield Blues Band** was first on the scene. It was started in Chicago (appropriately enough!) by its namesake singer-harmonica player. Growing up in the Windy City, Paul decided in his teens that he'd try to be the next Little Walter. It was the late 1950s and Chicago blues was in all its glory. Before he was old enough to drink, and before Caucasians were often seen in local blues clubs, young Paul was a novel addition to the scene.

At the University of Chicago Paul met Elvin Bishop, who'd grown up in Tulsa as a blues fan and played some fine straight-ahead electric blues guitar, and the two formed a band. A short while later gui-

THE PAUL BUTTERFIELD BLUES BAND

EAST/WEST

(Elektra 7315)

tarist Mike Bloomfield joined up. He was a rich kid from the 'burbs, two years younger than Paul and Elvin, who was amazing the patrons of those same blues clubs with his skilled and passionate lead playing. Organist Mark Naftalin, bassist Jerome Arnold and drummer Sam Lay (the latter two African-American) completed the band that made its debut LP for the folk label Elektra in 1965.

That first album was fairly basic Chicago electric blues, with a couple of differences: the listener is drawn to the instrumental work more than to the vocals (in black blues, the singing almost always takes center stage, however fine the musicians)…and the energy is geared for the excitement of listeners rather than dancers (in other words, the fast songs are faster). When the band toured, listeners were galvanized by the dueling guitars of Bloomfield and Bishop (and also because in many places the "Butterband" was the loudest music of any kind people had ever heard). A simple instrumental jam evolved into a monumental showpiece called "East/West," in which Bloomfield spun blues lines into free-form improvisations that almost resembled Indian ragas. A series of early 1966 shows in California made a huge impression on musicians in the Bay Area, whose "San Francisco Sound" would soon transform rock.

The *East/West* album, which also contained the band's most thunderous electric blues, proved to be a hard one to follow. Bloomfield left to form Electric Flag, a horn band that moved closer to the B.B. King paradigm. Interestingly, the Butterfield Band did the same, adding horns as Bishop reclaimed the lead guitar role with his more orthodox style. Though both Butterfield and Bloomfield produced more fine music after *East/West*, and Bloomfield played on the popular *Super Session* LP with rockers Al Kooper and Stephen Stills, neither man ever again created the kind of excitement they

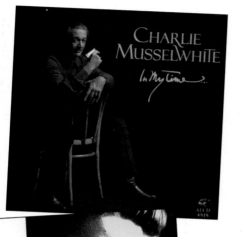

did in 1966. Both died tragically of drug overdoses. Bishop started his own band which fit nicely into the "Southern rock" wave of the 1970s, had a hit single with "Fooled Around and Fell In Love," signed with Alligator Records, and thrives today on the classic-rock circuit. Naftalin relocated to the Bay Area and became a pillar of the blues scene there. His radio shows and concert promotions have nourished the careers of many West Coast bluesmen.

Charlie Musselwhite (1944-) began his career in 1960s Chicago somewhat in Butterfield's shadows. While the latter soared and crashed, Musselwhite just kept at it and at it, and is finally getting some recognition as one of blues' very best hamonica men (and a fine singer and slide guitarist as well). Born in Mississippi, Charlie grew up in Memphis where Will Shade of the Memphis Jug Band gave him lessons. He moved to Chicago in 1962, busked at the city's famous Maxwell Street marketplace and started playing clubs, especially with singer-guitarist J.B. Hutto, and made his first LP for the folk label Vanguard Records in 1966. As with a remarkable number of veteran bluesmen, his music and career took on new life after signing with Alligator Records in 1990.

In Los Angeles, a group of folk musicians formed an electric blues band in early 1965 called The Rising Sons. Despite some magic moments on stage, the band never quite gelled, and its only album was not released until almost 30 years later. However, two members

CHARLIE MUSSELWHITE

THE BLUES NEVER DIE

(Vanguard 153/154)

IN MY TIME

(Alligator 4818)

In this newly recorded set, Musselwhite pays tribute to the artists that inspired him most—Little Walter, both Sonny Boy Williamsons, and many more, nicely demonstrating his own skill and versatility in the process.

would often be heard from again. Guitarist **Ry Cooder** went on to make solo albums and film soundtracks which often display his mastery of slide guitar and Blind Blake–style fingerpicking. And the Rising Sons' lead singer was **Taj Mahal**, the young African-American who revived and expanded the old songster tradition on his own long series of solo albums and remains a much-loved live performer.

The most commercially successful American blues band of the 1960s was **Canned Heat**, also started in Los Angeles in 1965. The lead singer was Bob Hite, nicknamed The Bear for his size. The Bear was a record collector; at age 20 he was reputed to have the best blues collection in L.A. He had never sung on stage, but he loved to sing along with his records. In 1965 he met Alan Wilson, who had come to L.A. from Boston to help acoustic guitarist John Fahey write his UCLA master's thesis on Charlie Patton. Wilson, then 22, had an encyclopedic knowledge of pre-WWII blues guitar; he had already accompanied Son House on his comeback album and had even taught House to play some songs he'd recorded but had forgotten. Wilson was also a John Lee Hooker fan, and played excellent Little Walter–style harmonica. Hite and Wilson started Canned Heat as an acoustic jug band; finding gigs scarce, they mutated into an electric band that soon attracted a following around L.A., especially for its

one-chord Hooker-style boogies which could go on for 20 minutes or more, whipping crowds into a frenzy.

The first Canned Heat LP was fairly orthodox. The second (*Boogie With Canned Heat*) contained a riproaring 11-minute boogie and also an Alan Wilson experiment: he took a rather obscure Chicago electric blues, Floyd Jones' "On the Road Again," re-wrote it as a one-chord boogie, sang it in a rich falsetto voice inspired by Skip James, and added a tamboura (the instrument that provides the drones behind Indian ragas—another form of one-chord music). Wilson sang and played all the parts except bass and drums. The result was not only hauntingly beautiful, it was a hit single that made Canned Heat big-time rock stars.

The followup *Living the Blues* was a double album with a boogie that was probably the lengthiest blues ever recorded—40 minutes. It also had another miraculous Wilson creation based on the antique sound of Texas songster Henry Thomas and his pan-pipes; Thomas' "Bull Doze Blues" became "Goin' Up The Country," another hit single.

Alan Wilson was an unlikely rock star. Intellectual, highly introverted, extremely nearsighted (thus his nickname "Blind Owl", he stood absolutely still on stage when performing. In September 1970, Alan died in his sleeping bag in the backyard of Hite's Topanga Canyon home. Rumors of drugs and suicide to the contrary, he apparently died of an aneurysm caused by injuries in an earlier auto accident. Alan Wilson was 27; we'll never know what wondrous music he took with him. The Bear carried on until 1981 when he died of an overdose. Drummer Fito de la Parra continues the band to this day, playing fine blues—but Alan Wilson was irreplaceable.

Two other white bands that attracted attention in the mid-to-late 1960s: New York's **Blues Project**, notable for its fast-fingered young musicians and its frequent arguments about whether to be a blues band or something else (two members left to form the very popular Blood, Sweat & Tears), and Chicago's **Siegel-Schwall Band**, which made a dozen albums includ-

CANNED HEAT

UNCANNED! THE BEST OF CANNED HEAT

(EMI 29165)

ing the much-debated *Three Pieces for Blues Band and Symphony Orchestra* (1971).

In 1969, with thunderous hype from Columbia Records, the world was introduced to the blues of **Johnny Winter** (1944-), the photogenic albino guitarist/singer from Texas. Columbia had won a bidding war for Winter's services, convinced that he was America's answer to Eric Clapton. Winter, then 25, had played both rock and blues back in Texas, but visits to Chicago (where he played with Mike Bloomfield) and London convinced him that blues was the way to go…and it was Winter's blues that convinced Columbia to put nearly $500,000 in his pocket. One wonders what Willie Dixon and "Shakey" Horton thought about all that as they backed Winter up on one track of the debut LP.

Regardless, Winter turned out to be an excellent blues player (whose occasional tendency to overkill only made him more appealing to rock fans, just as with Clapton in 1969) and a credible singer. In the 1970s he played more rock than blues (especially after his brother Edgar became a rock star) but earned blues lovers' gratitude by reviving Muddy Waters' career with brilliant production on the great man's final LPs. Winter's own blues came back into focus with several Alligator albums in the 1980s.

We must mention one more white blues artist whose career began in the late 1960s. **Bonnie Raitt** (1949-) was not exactly born with blues; her father is Broadway musical comedy star John Raitt. Nevertheless she got hooked on blues as a teenager, was an excellent singer and slide guitarist by the time she was 20, and soon became an East Coast folk club favorite. There's some nice blues here and there on her

first few Warner Bros. albums, but the company preferred her as a pop singer, and that's how she's made her living ever since, though she's never stopped singing or supporting blues.

◆

It's not hard to see why Warner Bros. steered Bonnie Raitt away from blues. Blues darn near died in the early 1970s. The white electric blues scene, so full of momentum in the 1960s, fizzled quickly as many of its stars shifted their energies to corporate rock and pop, while others struggled with heroin and other drugs. The black acoustic players from before World War II were dying off, and the electric stars found good gigs and record deals harder to come by as their original audience aged.

Blues may have looked dead on arrival in the 1970s...but a few good people still felt its heart beating. B.B. and Muddy kept on touring, the Europeans still knew a good thing when they heard it, the Ann Arbor blues festival gathered the faithful every year, and in Chicago there was a new one-man record label called Alligator. One by one, people started coming back to all that music that seems so sad but makes you feel so happy.

JOHNNY WINTER

SCORCHIN' BLUES

(Columbia 52466)

Chapter 10
Blues Today

Many people worked long and hard, on stage and behind the scenes, to bring blues back to where it is today. People have devoted hours, days, years, their lives to the cause, satisfied with small rewards: another month's rent paid, a thousand albums sold, a show where old fans and new had a great time, a new wheelchair for a living legend, Blues Day at the junior high school.

Of course, nothing helps sell tickets or CDs like the perception that something is a hit. In the 1970s, the prevailing wisdom was that blues was a has-been. Blues had been great, but it was out of fashion, its day was past.

Enter Stevie Ray Vaughan.

◆

Stephen Ray Vaughan was the younger of two guitar-playing sons of a white Dallas working-class family. His father's parents had been sharecroppers, like so many rural black families of their generation.

The older son, **Jimmie Vaughan** (1951-) co-founded **The Fabulous Thunderbirds** in 1974 with singer-harmonica player Kim Wilson. The T-Birds soon became a mainstay of the small but lively blues scene in Austin, Texas. When the band eventually released an album in 1979, it was acclaimed as the best authentic Chicago-style blues by a white band since the heyday of Butterfield and Canned Heat a decade earlier.

Jimmie Vaughan began playing guitar as a boy. At age 15 he was good enough to join The Chessmen, the most popular Top 40 cover band in town. They were big enough to open for Jimi Hendrix (whose playing blew Jimmie's mind as it did everybody's) but had difficulty handling the pressures that came with

THE FABULOUS THUNDERBIRDS

HOT STUFF—THE GREATEST HITS
(Epic/Associated 53007)

local stardom. When The Chessmen broke up, Jimmie formed Texas Storm (later simply Storm). Janis Joplin saw the band in 1968 and invited them to the West Coast where her enthusiasm stirred up record company interest, but it was soon evident that these teenagers weren't quite prepared to be rock stars. Not long after that episode, Jimmie saw Muddy Waters play in Dallas and decided he'd rather be a starving bluesman than a rich rocker anyway. He moved to Austin in 1970, lured by the capital city's fledgling blues scene, and eventually formed the Thunderbirds with Wilson.

Stevie Ray Vaughan (1954-1990) shared Jimmie's record collection ("Wham," a 1963 instrumental 45 by Lonnie Mack, was an early favorite) and his taste for hard-core electric blues—but the two only occasionally played together. Stevie wasn't as sociable as his brother, or as good looking, but he had an ideal physique for a guitarist—muscular forearms and huge hands. He could play with heavier strings (for a ballsier sound) and bend them further than anyone else around. Like his brother, he learned from R&B records, which he'd slow down and play over and over until he'd perfected every lick. He heard Jimi Hendrix, and was even more transformed than his brother had been.

Like Jimmie, Stevie began playing in local bands at 15. One of these bands had enough local success to convince Stevie he was wasting his time in high school. He quit in the middle of his senior year, and moved to Austin where his brother was. He briefly joined a half dozen bands, even making a jaunt to L.A. with a band called the Nightcrawlers assembled by Marc Benno, a singer-songwriter who had a deal with A&M Records. (The album they made went unreleased.)

Eventually he got an invitation to join the slickest and most popular club band in town, The Cobras. He stayed for two years, playing R&B favorites from the Wilson Pickett, Junior Parker and Bobby Bland songbooks, with an occasional harder blues thrown in. With the Cobras, he sang for the first time, a song or two per set at first, more than that after the lead singer came down with nodes on his larynx. His favorite song to sing was "Texas Flood," a mournful slow blues recorded by the little-known Larry Davis for Duke Records in 1958.

That song would remain a favorite throughout his career. He was taking his first steps toward stardom.

Meanwhile, Austin got its first full-time blues club. Antone's reminded him that blues was his first love, and his next band was a blues band. It was a joint venture with a charismatic local singer named Lou Ann Barton, called Triple Threat Revue. She would sing the first half of the set, then turn the spotlight over to Stevie who would sing blues and play some Freddie King or Albert Collins instrumentals.

Triple Threat, which soon downsized to Double Trouble (after an Otis Rush song), established Stevie's rep as a guitarslinger all over Texas, and turned many a head elsewhere—but after a year the band was just barely paying its way. It was the zenith of disco and

New Wave, and guitar blues bands were passé—or so they heard, again and again.

Lou Ann Barton could only take so much of that, and quit the band after an especially discouraging gig at New York's Lone Star Cafe.

Stevie, at last, had his own band, and could play what he pleased—still hardcore blues, but with more and more Hendrix creeping into the mix, more and more excursions into electronic wonderland within the context of a blues solo, and a few actual Hendrix songs like "Manic Depression" or "Voodoo Chile (Slight Return)."

Soon they were Hot. Jackson Browne heard them and offered them three days of studio time to do an album. David Bowie heard them and wanted Stevie to play on his new album, which he did (*Let's Dance*, a great success), and to join his band, which he almost did before deciding he had to be loyal to Double Trouble and to the blues. Double Trouble did a showcase in New York for the Rolling Stones. Mick Jagger and the other members of that one-time London blues band were suitably blown away, but decided not to sign Double Trouble to their record label—a blues band wouldn't sell, they said. To add insult to injury, blues specialists Alligator Records also turned the band down—it wasn't pure enough for them.

Sometimes just one "yes" is all you need, though, and Double Trouble finally got a good one. John Hammond, the veteran producer at CBS Records, had been courted by Stevie's management for some time, and finally gave the green light after his son, singer John Hammond Jr., gave his endorsement. The tapes made at Jackson Browne's became the first LP, which was titled *Texas Flood*, released in the summer of 1983 and eventually went platinum (one million copies sold). The following summer, *Couldn't Stand the Weather* did even better. The heat even rubbed off on Jimmie Vaughan, whose Fabulous Thunderbirds had a Top Ten single with "Tuff Enuff" in 1986.

Stevie had all the money he could spend—and before long, more drugs than even he could handle. Since his days with The Cobras he had been famous for being able to sing and play all day and all night with boundless energy and creativity despite an equally boundless intake of cocaine and alcohol. When he wanted coke while on stage, he'd simply dissolve some in his Crown Royal. The body can only take so much, and his performances eventually did begin to suffer. On tour in Switzerland, he hit bottom. It didn't take him long to realize what he had to do, and with the help of further treatment and Alcoholics Anonymous he learned how to live clean with the same energy he'd put into learning guitar.

He emerged in 1987 clean and sober, much more sociable than before, and playing as well as he ever had if not better. Soon Double Trouble was back on the road as if nothing had happened. He made a fine new album, *In Step*.

Meanwhile, brother Jimmie was getting bored with the Fabulous Thunderbirds, and had decided to follow his brother into a sober lifestyle. One thing led to another, and soon Jimmie and Stevie committed themselves to making music together for the first time, launching the partnership with a superb album. *Family Style* by "The Vaughan Brothers" was not the guitar war the fans might have expected, but a light-hearted jump blues romp.

Stevie decided to disband Double Trouble, at least temporarily, and hit the road with Jimmie and a new band—but there were a few more Double Trouble gigs on the schedule. The band was second-billed for an Eric Clapton concert, also featuring Buddy Guy, on a foggy night at an outdoor arena at a Wisconsin ski area for 30,000 fans. After the triumphant show, Stevie boarded a helicopter for a ride to Chicago, 90 miles away. The copter had only been aloft in the fog for a few seconds before it slammed into a ski slope, killing all aboard instantly. It was August 27, 1990; Stevie Ray Vaughan was 35.

There are many today who still maintain Stevie Ray Vaughan was the best blues guitarist that ever lived. True, some traditionalists thought his music was a bit over the top, his fast blues too fast and his slow blues too slow. However, the whole blues world benefitted immeasurably from his stardom. Millions who heard him on rock radio were introduced or re-introduced to blues through him, and became blues fans

STEVIE RAY VAUGHAN

TEXAS FLOOD
(Epic 38734)

COULDN'T STAND THE WEATHER
(Epic 39304)

IN STEP
(Epic 45024)

BOOK: STEVIE RAY VAUGHAN — CAUGHT IN THE CROSSFIRE
(1993 - Little, Brown)
An extensively researched, well written biography.

who bought blues albums and went to blues clubs and festivals. By the time of his death, blues had regained all the momentum it had lost in the 1970s, and a lot more; it was indeed bigger than ever. All that new life may well have been Stevie Ray's greatest gift to the music he loved so much.

◆

The long stretch between the Butterfield-Canned Heat era and the rise of the Vaughans was not totally devoid of white blues activity. **Roomful of Blues** started in Rhode Island way back in 1967, gradually progressed from a bar band to a measure of national renown, and has lasted over 30 years at this writing. The band has always specialized in jump blues, with horns—a genre widely scorned in the 1960s by those who preferred slide guitars and harmonicas—and has done a lot to make jump blues respectable. Roomful specializes in backing up veteran singers, having made albums with Joe Turner, Eddie "Cleanhead" Vinson and Earl King. Roomful of Blues has a couple of Vaughan connections: Lou Ann Barton sang with ROB before joining Stevie Ray, and ROB founder-guitarist Duke Robillard replaced Jimmie in the Fabulous Thunderbirds.

George Thorogood and the Destroyers began in Delaware in the early 1970s and signed with Rounder Records in 1977 as the respected folk label's first electric act, mixing solid blues with updated rockabilly to become pioneers of the now crowded

ROOMFUL OF BLUES

THE FIRST ALBUM

(32 Records 32003)

UNDER ONE ROOF

(Bullseye 9569)

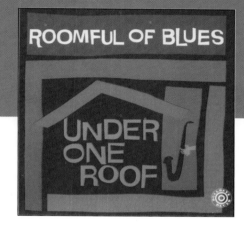

"retro-rock" genre. They made FM playlists in the next two years with Amos Milburn's "One Scotch, One Bourbon, One Beer" and Hank Williams' "Move It On Over" and solidified their place with constant touring (they once played all 50 states on 50 consecutive nights). "Bad To The Bone" took them to the next level in 1982 and remains an album-rock favorite.

'Gator Tales

Behind the scenes, one man who doesn't sing or play a note has done more to build the blues revival than most of the people who do. His name is **Bruce Iglauer** and he owns **Alligator Records**, first and

GEORGE THOROGOOD

THE BADDEST OF GEORGE THOROGOOD AND THE DESTROYERS

(EMI 97718)

largest of the now numerous independent blues record labels.

When Iglauer arrived in Chicago in 1970, blues was down, way down, but not out. He soon found inspiration at a rickety little South Side tavern, where a singer-slide guitarist named Theodore Roosevelt **"Hound Dog" Taylor** (1917-75) packed the house and rocked the house every Sunday afternoon with his stomp-down Mississippi blues. The rest of the world was missing out on a great party, Iglauer thought, and he'd have to fix that.

He became Hound Dog's booking agent, road manager and cheering section…and when no one else would record Hound Dog, he started a record company to do that, and called it Alligator. The LP sold 10,000 copies, a smash by early 1970s blues standards, which was a good thing because Iglauer had put his life savings into it.

When the distributors got around to paying

him, he could make another album, which turned out to be a set by harmonica veteran Big Walter Horton and a younger harp player, **Carey Bell**. Album three was by **Son Seals**, an Arkansas-born singer-guitarist who like Bell had arrived in Chicago too late to get in on the local scene's glory days, but had a regular following at one of the few remaining hot spots. Seals was 31 when Iglauer first

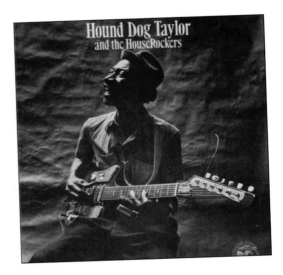

HOUND DOG TAYLOR

HOUND DOG TAYLOR AND THE HOUSEROCKERS

(Alligator 4701)

recorded him; over the next decade he would become one of the city's top bluesmen, often compared to the late Magic Sam for his aggressive, piercing guitar leads.

In the studio, the bottom line had to be watched, of course, but once Alligator had committed itself to an artist, the only aim was to present the artist's artistry as fully as possible. It was quite a difference from the way records had usually been made in Chicago—haphazardly in the early days, in cookie-cutter fashion in the Lester Melrose days, more creatively but not always with the artist's best interests in mind in the Chess days. In Alligator's early days, Iglauer's commitment often extended to booking and managing the artists—anything to help them get their careers off the ground.

Alligator's first "name" artist was **Koko Taylor**, who had been a Chess Records star in the 1960s. (More on Koko in the "Soul Blues" section.) Now the label had momentum, and began to look outside Chicago for great artists who needed recording. **Albert Collins** hadn't recorded for eight years when Iglauer looked him up, but still sounded as great as ever. His first Alligator album, with more emphasis on vocals than before, rejuvenated his career.

Showdown!

In 1986, Albert took part in the most famous Alligator album of all, so far: *Showdown!*. Featuring Collins along with fellow singer-guitarists Johnny Copeland and Robert Cray, it sold well into six figures and hugely helped the careers of all three men. (More on Copeland and Cray a bit later.)

The album proclaimed, loud and clear, that there was more to modern blues guitar than the brothers Vaughan. No Hendrix tricks here, and there actually isn't all that much flash for flash's sake…just strong, strong solos that build and build. Nothing cute at all—it's as serious as John Wayne, very macho. The musicians respect each other enough to stay out of each other's way. (The one and only double lead chorus, by Collins and Copeland, is a real treat.)

There are contrasts between the guitarists… Collins with his trademark ice-picking, Copeland with his hard slashing, Cray a bit more melodic…but the similarities are greater, each man enhancing in his own way the lead-guitar mode that started with T-Bone, was nurtured by B.B. and began to dominate blues in the late 1950s.

The name on the album signified conflict—war gets more ink than peace, after all—but *Showdown!* was very much a solid team effort, each man helping the others do their very best.

"Rejuvenated…career" were two words that appeared in the bio of many a bluesman and blueswoman from that point on, thanks to Alligator: Lonnie Brooks, James Cotton, Clifton Chenier, Lazy Lester, Johnny Winter, Roy Buchanan, Charlie Musselwhite, Lonnie Mack. Professor Longhair would be on that list, but he died on the very day Alligator released what would be hailed as his finest album, *Crawfish Fiesta*.

ALBERT COLLINS, JOHNNY COPELAND, ROBERT CRAY

SHOWDOWN!

(Alligator 4743)

No Alligator artist enjoyed a more rewarding career turnaround than **Luther Allison** (1939-1997), a top-drawer West Side Chicago singer-guitarist who came along just a year or two too late to catch the original Electric Chicago scene at the peak of its momentum. Born in Arkansas, he moved with his family to Chicago in 1952, started his first blues band in 1957, and took over Freddie King's band in 1959 when the latter moved on. By the early 1960s he was one of the city's top live blues acts, but didn't record an album until 1969's *Love Me Mama* for Delmark. His live shows promoting this LP on the East and West Coasts and at the Ann Arbor Blues Festival were much acclaimed, and he was signed by Motown Records which had previously all but ignored blues. Alas, his 1970s work for Motown and other labels failed to advance his career, while annoying the hardcore blues fans of the day with his ventures into rock and soul.

Like so many bluesmen before him, Luther moved to Europe and found a much warmer reception, enjoying a nice career there while being all but forgotten back home. Touring the Continent steadily, he built a reputation as a searing guitarist, a deep and soulful singer, and a tireless non-

LONNIE MACK

STRIKE LIKE LIGHTNING

(Alligator 4739)

stop showman. In 1994 Alligator decided he was ripe for a revival of his American career. Within a year Luther was the hottest blues act in the nation. He practically swept the W.C. Handy Awards and all the other major blues awards in 1996 and 1997, with three Alligator CDs riding the crest of the wave. Luther was widely hailed as the greatest live performer on the scene, and deeply mourned when he died August 12, 1997 at age 57, just a few weeks after being diagnosed with lung cancer.

◆

And now a word about the other two stars on *Showdown*. **Johnny Copeland** (1937-1997) knew Albert Collins from way back;

he too began his career in Houston. In his twenties (the late 1950s and early 1960s) he tried hard to make it as a mainstream R&B artist, without much success. In his late thirties he moved to New York City, declared himself a bluesman, and was widely recognized as one of the best soon after he began recording for Rounder in 1980.

The third man on *Showdown!* has become the most famous of all, vanguard of a new generation of bluesmen. **Robert Cray** (1953-) was born in Georgia but raised here, there and everywhere—his dad was a military man. Eventually the family settled in Tacoma, Wash. He didn't hear much blues until Albert Collins came through town one night. Sixteen-year-old Robert instantly became a blues fan and soon began playing blues as well.

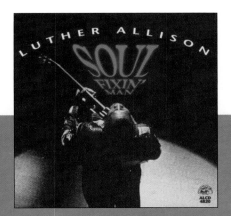

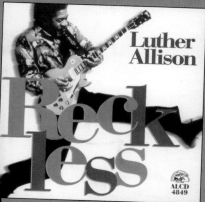

LUTHER ALLISON

SOUL FIXIN' MAN

(Alligator 4820)

BLUE STREAK

(Alligator 4834)

RECKLESS

(Alligator 4849)

"When Will It Change" is one of the surprisingly few blues that directly addresses the issue of racial discrimination.

In 1974 Robert portrayed a bass player in the film *Animal House* (he's one of Otis Day's Knights). More to the point, The Robert Cray Band was becoming well known locally, and began recording a few years later. By the time he hooked up with old friend Albert Collins for *Showdown!*, he had three LPs out and was gathering some national attention. In 1986, following *Showdown!*, Robert signed with a major label and released *Strong Persuader*. This became a massive national hit, receiving heavy airplay on FM rock stations that hadn't played anything by a black man since Hendrix, and spawning a hit single, "Smoking Gun." Like Stevie Ray Vaughan's albums, *Strong Persuader* reached a great many people who wouldn't have considered themselves blues fans, and made many new blues fans in the process. It sold more copies than any other album by a black bluesman up to that time (excepting only Hendrix).

Strong Persuader is not, of course, "pure" blues by any pre-existing standards. There's a lot of soul influence, and some rock, and the production has a certain gloss to it. And one might notice that the other members of the Robert Cray Band are all Caucasian. But blues never was that "pure" anyway, if you take a good long look at it! Call *Strong Persuader* another evolutionary landmark, and call Robert Cray a superstar.

'Possum Chops

There are dozens of small independent labels making blues CDs today. While pleasures abound on these CDs, others are little more than demos for local bands, produced on a shoestring budget without much imagination.

JOHNNY COPELAND

WHEN THE RAIN STARTS FALLIN'

(Rounder 11515)
A compilation of highlights from Copeland's earlier Rounder LP's.

AIN'T NOTHING BUT A PARTY

(Rounder 205)

Fat Possum Records of Oxford, Mississippi also works on shoestring budgets, but the results are something else. Fat Possum records 75-year-old back-country blues scufflers like they were 15-year-old punk rockers. The cruder and rawer, the better. In a word, Fat Possum has attitude. This is a label that titled one of its samplers "Not The Same Old Blues Crap."

The whole thing started in the late 1980s when Matt Johnson, a University of Mississippi grad student, drove out to the backwoods to find some music. At Junior Kimbrough's juke joint in Holly Springs, Johnson had the same sort of epiphany Bruce Iglauer had had in Chicago two decades earlier. With a little help from some friends, he started Fat Possum in 1991 to record Kimbrough and another local old-timer, R.L. Burnside. It grew from there to a label with a 20-artist roster of artists from many places, all making raw, wild, wonderful music with no regard for decorum.

For Burnside's 1998 release *Come On In*, Fat Possum brought in producer Tom Rothrock, best known for his work with alt-rocker Beck. *Come On In* sounds not unlike Beck's "Loser," using repeated samples as part of its funky, minimalist mix. Traditionalists were predictably outraged…but if blues is going to stay as vigorous and vital as it is, and not become as ossi-

ROBERT CRAY

STRONG PERSUADER

(Mercury 830 568)

DON'T BE AFRAID OF THE DARK

(Mercury 834 923)

fied as Dixieland, it can use a few shots of attitude.

◆

A few more blues stars who illuminate the start of blues' second century: **Joe Louis Walker** (1949-) grew up in San Francisco, and as a teenager got to know Mike

Bloomfield, who had moved there after leaving the Butterfield Blues Band. With Bloomfield's help the young Walker learned Chicago-style lead guitar.* A series of albums for the Bay Area–based Hightone label (where Robert Cray also got his start) made Walker nationally known, and he's now one of blues' biggest draws. His recent CDs for the Verve label (a unit of giant Polygram) are elaborate affairs with lots of guest stars and complex multi-studio production, but the feeling is what counts, and it's there. Walker's blues is right in today's mainstream—soul blues mostly, enlivened by some nice contemporary jazz touches in the guitar and occasional excursions into more traditional territory.

The late **William Clarke** (1951-1996) was the finest younger harmonica player in blues at the time of his death at age 45 from heart failure. A Caucasian,

---

* There's a certain historical symmetry in the fact that Bloomfield, a white man, was a blues mentor for the younger African-American Walker.

JOE LOUIS WALKER

LIVE AT SLIM'S, Vol. 1
(Hightone 8025)

JLW
(Verve-Gitanes 314 523 118)

he grew up in a Los Angeles suburb, haunting blues clubs in the L.A. ghetto and becoming a student and protegé of George "Harmonica" Smith, who had earlier been a member of Muddy Waters' band. Two albums on a small local label got him a deal with Alligator Records; the four albums he made there are textbooks in the art of harmonica playing, especially the larger, deeper chromatic harmonica. In addition to traditional Chicago blues, he liked to play West Coast jump, with the harmonica taking the place of the horn section. His final CD, *The Hard Way*, has several tracks inspired by the organ-and-sax jazz trios of the 1960s.

Kenny Wayne Shepherd (1977-) became the blues prodigy of 1996 with his CD *Ledbetter Heights*, which put the blond 19-year-old at the top of the *Billboard* blues charts for five months. He became familiar to rock audiences as well with heavy FM airplay and opening gigs for The Eagles and Bob Dylan. The son of Shreveport radio personality Ken Shepherd, "KWS" is heir apparent to Stevie Ray Vaughan, whom his father introduced him to when Kenny was 7. His playing has much of Stevie Ray's flash and virtuosity, and occasional tendency to excess (which of course hasn't hurt him one bit with rock audiences). On Bukka White's song "Aberdeen," he plays Bukka's original guitar arrangement very nicely for a few choruses before lighting the afterburners and rocking out. Shepherd does not sing, leaving the lead vocals to others. That does confound people's expectations of what a bluesman (or a rock

WILLIAM CLARKE

BLOWIN' LIKE HELL

(Alligator 4788)

THE HARD WAY

(Alligator 4842)

star) should be, but one remembers that Stevie Ray did not sing that early in his career, and neither did Eric Clapton.

As this book goes to press, **Susan Tedeschi** (1970-) is blues' hottest new artist. Born and raised near Boston, Tedeschi (tuh-DES-kee) sings originals and standards and plays electric lead guitar. She's a traditionalist, influenced much more by 1950s and 1960s electric blues than by soul blues or anything else happening today. Yet her CD *Just Won't Burn* was a huge hit on "adult alternative" radio, more evidence of the seemingly endless appeal of superbly performed "basic" blues. She won the 2000 W.C. Handy Award for Female Contemporary Artist of the Year.

◆

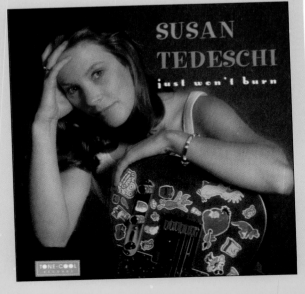

KENNY WAYNE SHEPHERD

LEDBETTER HEIGHTS

(Giant 24621)

SUSAN TEDESCHI

JUST WON'T BURN

(Tone-Cool TC 1164)

Soul Blues

Soul Blues (n.) Blues with elements derived from the soul music genre, including gospel-style singing, frequent use of horns, and harmonic structures other than 12-bar blues, including structures borrowed from gospel and pop. Soul blues is the basis of Jonny Lang's music.

Before the 1950s soul blues would have been unthinkable. Blues was the devil's music, and to sing it in church style would have been blasphemy. Of course that dichotomy didn't stop church music from borrowing ideas from blues ("why should the devil have all the good tunes," etc.) but it didn't work the other way. Gospel singing, with its stirring crescendos, its frenzied shouts, its gravel-voiced high notes, and its melismas (cascades of notes sung to a single syllable) stayed in the church.

Then along came B.B. King. There's a hint of gospel tone and phrasing in his first hit, 1951's "3 O'Clock Blues"; it was one of the main things that made King stand out from other bluesmen of the time (along with his guitar playing, of course). By the time you get to "The Thrill Is Gone" (1969), there's a lot of church in his voice.

The Chicago West Side bluesmen of the late 1950s, expanding on what B.B. started, put even more church in their voices (especially those frenzied, raspy high notes) while shifting the guitar into overdrive.

Meanwhile, the genre of soul music was getting started. Ray Charles, who began as a bluesman, all but invented the genre, pretty much leaving blues behind in the process. Other soul pioneers—Jackie Wilson, Wilson Pickett, Otis Redding, Aretha Franklin—never were blues singers. Young black audiences in the 1960s didn't want to hear the slightest trace of blues, and few blues singers managed to cross over into soul.

One who did was Bobby Bland, who had a lot of church in his voice from the start. His hits in the late 1950s and 1960s effectively straddled the line between soul and blues. His large audience, predominantly black, female and over 30, loved soul music but did not turn its back on blues like younger people did.

Koko Taylor (Cora Walton, 1935-) was another soul blues pioneer. After beginning her recording career (as Cocoa Taylor) with vaudeville blues veteran

Victoria Spivey's record label, she was discovered by Willie Dixon who sang background on her 1966 breakthrough hit, "Wang Dang Doodle" (which he'd written five years earlier for Howlin' Wolf). (The flip side of the 45 was "Blues Heaven," after which Dixon's charitable foundation was named.)

Born to a sharecropper family, she moved to Chicago at age 18 and worked as a maid while often visiting local blues clubs, where she began sitting in with the stars and very gradually working her way up to top billing. She recorded for Chess until the label was sold, then signed with Alligator in 1974—by far the best known artist on the label at that point. Since then she's reigned as Queen of the Blues, winning more W.C. Handy Awards through the years than any other artist.

Her style has a bit in common with Willie Mae "Big Mama" Thornton's, with all its antecedents going back to 1920s vaudeville blues. It's churchier, though...and Koko has been a lot more sympathetically recorded than Big Mama was. Today the W.C. Handy Awards directors classify her as "contemporary blues" rather than "soul blues," perhaps because of her accompaniments and the Alligator affiliation; there's certainly no one more soulful in blues than Koko Taylor.

Chess Records' biggest soul blues star int he 1960s was singer-guitarist **Little Milton** (Milton Campbell, 1934-). Born in Mississippi, he recorded for Sun and Meteor in Memphis before moving to St. Louis and recording for the local Bobbin label from 1957 to 1960, while building career momentum through con-

**KOKO TAYLOR:
WHAT IT TAKES—
THE CHESS YEARS**

(MCA-Chess 9328)

I GOT WHAT IT TAKES

(Alligator 4706)

JUMP FOR JOY

(Alligator 4784)

stant touring. Moving to Chess' Checker label in 1961, he had a #1 R&B hit in 1965 with "We're Gonna Make It" and a total of 17 chart singles during his ten-year stay there.

Little Johnny Taylor (Johnny Young, 1943-) is a soul blues star today, though he's still best known for an emotion-soaked slow blues he recorded in 1963 for the San Francisco–based Galaxy label, "Part Time Love." Raised in Los Angeles, he was a member of gospel's famous Mighty Clouds of Joy in the 1950s before switching to blues. He's not to be confused with **Johnnie Taylor** (1938-2000), who succeeded Sam Cooke as lead singer of the Soul Stirrers before making a string of soul hits including "Who's Making Love" and "Disco Lady."

Just as Alligator Records helped shake the blues revival out of its doldrums, a Jackson, Mississippi, label called Malaco Records revived soul blues in the early 1980s. Malaco's breakthrough was an album called *Down Home* by **Z.Z. Hill** (Arzell Hill, 1935-1984). Hill had been a marginally successful soul singer for over 15 years before signing with Malaco. The key track was "Down Home Blues." A blues song about a woman who loved blues, it carried the message that blues was OK. (One is reminded just a bit of all those country & western songs about how wonderful old time country music is.) The Southern audience loved it so much that Hill, all but unknown outside the South, might have been the most popular bluesman in all African America at the time of his death following a 1984 car smash. (Rockers Z.Z. Top appropriated his initials.)

Malaco Records has continued to thrive on soul blues, with such artists as the late Johnny Taylor (the "Disco Lady" man) and Little Milton. Ichiban Records of Atlanta works similar territory with Little Johnnie Taylor (the "Part Time Love" man) and **Clarence Carter** (1936-), whose deliciously salacious "Strokin'" is quite a change from his late 1960s–early 1970s hits like "Slip Away" and "Patches." **Otis Clay** (1942-) is one of quite a few second-tier 1960s soul singers who have recently found new life as 1990s soul bluesmen.

Strictly speaking, much of today's "soul blues" is still more soul than blues, but with revival audiences becoming less purist all the time, artists like these have shown up more and more on festival programs, reminding us again of the power of the human voice.

WE'RE GONNA MAKE IT: LITTLE MILTON SINGS BIG BLUES

(Chess CHD 5906)

Z. Z. HILL: DOWN HOME

(Malaco 7406)

Esther and Etta

A word or three about two great singers often categorized as "soul blues," though their music and especially their background is different from others in that class.

Esther Phillips (Esther Mae Jones, 1935-1984) became "Little Esther," R&B's top teen idol of the early 1950s, when she joined Johnny Otis' band after winning a talent contest. She was still only 14 when her vocal on Otis' "Double Crossing Blues" took the record to Number One on the R&B singles charts. This and its many followups were West Coast–style jump blues enlivened by her sharp, sassy singing, admired by all for its maturity but not yet what we'd call "soulful."

Church got into her music a little later, after she'd clawed her way back from a long struggle with heroin addiction that began not long after her first hits. Though not blues, her 1962 cover of the country song "Release Me" is as heartbreakingly thrilling as soul music gets. She recorded frequently in the 1960s before relapsing into addiction, then had another comeback in the 1970s.

Etta James (1938-) became R&B's teen idol of the *late* 1950s, again with the help of Johnny Otis. When Hank Ballard's risqué "Work With Me Annie" became one of the top R&B hits of 1954, James and Otis wrote and recorded the answer song "Roll With Me Henry" (retitled "The Wallflower" to deflect criticism from guardians of morality), which became almost as big a hit as the original (and even bigger, if you count Georgia Gibbs' bowdlerized cover, "Dance With Me Henry".)

James had even more success in the 1960s with Chess' Argo label. This was when the church got into her voice a little more. She was equally influenced, though, by the great jazz ballad singers like Billie Holiday and Dinah Washington. She, too, was alleged to have drug problems at one time. Recently she's found a home in the soul blues genre; repeatedly winning the W.C. Handy Award as female Soul Blues artist of the year.

**LITTLE ESTHER PHILLIPS
THE BEST OF ESTER PHILLIPS
(1962-1970)**

(Rhino 72624)

**ETTA JAMES:
R&B DYNAMITE**

(Flair/Virgin 91695)
Her 50s hits.

**HER GREATEST SIDES,
Vol. 1**

(MCA-Chess 9110)

Acoustic Blues—Redux

With the blues revival as big as it is currently, there's room in it for practically every imaginable style of blues—including something a lot of people thought they'd never see, a new group of young black acoustic blues singers.

For years and years **Taj Mahal** (Henry Fredericks, 1942-) had this niche practically all to himself. After leaving the mostly-white electric blues band The Rising Sons in 1966, Taj was signed as a solo artist by Columbia Records. He made a series of tasty LPs of primarily acoustic music for Columbia, mixing traditional blues with other folksongs. His score for the 1972 film *Sounder*, a landmark in the portrayal of African-American life on screen, gained Taj a lot of respect; he also acted in the movie. Taj has continued to record eclectic, flavorful potpourris of blues, reggae and other black sounds, including ventures

into R&B, and often appears at blues festivals.

Alligator Records, which recorded electric blues exclusively in its earlier years, has tested the new acoustic waters lately with fine results. **Saffire—The Uppity Blues Women** is acoustic in a slightly different sense: this interracial female trio uses piano, guitar and bass to back up their broad repertoire of originals and covers, many of which bring back the spirit and sound of urban blues of the 1930s or even 1920s vaudeville blues, but with the modern sensibility you'd expect from their name. **Cephas & Wiggins** carry on the sweet and lively spirit and sound of Brownie McGhee and Sonny Terry and the Piedmont legends who preceded them. John Cephas was born in 1930 but didn't become an active bluesman until the 1970s, when he joined the younger Phil

**TAJ MAHAL:
TAJ'S BLUES**

(Columbia 52465)

Wiggins. After some CDs for the Flying Fish folk label (including the Handy Award–winning *Dog Days of August*), the duo signed with Alligator. They sing originals and older blues, including a good many songs not originally associated with the Piedmont but fitting splendidly into that style.

Corey Harris (1969-) grew up in Denver, went to college in Maine, and now lives in New Orleans. He woodshedded his music, though, in the African nation of Cameroon where he was studying the local language on a research grant, with a box of blues cassettes from home to keep him company. A bottleneck specialist, he plays a guitar with an internal resonator, like the ones Tampa Red and Blind Boy Fuller played. He sings and plays blues from the 1950s and earlier, mixing elements from the original arrangements with his own appealing style. Now and then he sneaks in a lick inspired by some other kind of music he's heard, or a phrase from hip-hop (which is the grandson of blues poetry, after all). *Between Midnight and Day*, his first CD, was recorded with guitar only in one six-hour session (the way they often did it in the old days). *Fish Ain't Bitin'* has more originals, some sung with a brass trio that gives the music a marvelously old-timey yet innovative sound.

**COREY HARRIS:
BETWEEN MIDNIGHT
AND DAY**

(Alligator 4837)

FISH AIN'T BITIN'

(Alligator 4850)

KEB' MO

(OKeh 57863)

JUST LIKE YOU

(OKeh 67316)

KEB' MO: SLOW DOWN

(Sony 69376)

Keb' Mo (Kevin Moore, ca. 1952-) plays a guitar similar to Corey Harris', but his music is quite different. As a singer-songwriter his main influence appears to be contemporary soul blues, but he's turned down the volume and the intensity to bring out the beauty of his melodies and the poetry of his lyrics. With a discreet rhythm section on most tracks, the accompaniment is a perfect match. Along with his originals, which now and then venture into older acoustic blues styles, his CDs include some refreshingly innovative Robert Johnson covers. He signed with OKeh Records, CBS' 1990s revival of the label that made the first blues record back in 1920. His first CD won the W.C. Handy Award for best acoustic blues album in 1995. Recently he's added more electric sounds to his music.

Guy Davis (ca. 1956-) is more of a traditionalist, quite close in spirit to the acoustic revivalists of the 1960s. He's the kind of artist who'd like you to know the story behind each song, be it a classic from the pre-WWII era or one of his often quite poetic originals. He is the son of actors Ossie Davis and Ruby Dee.

GUY DAVIS: CALL DOWN THE THUNDER

(Red House 89)

BUTT NAKED FREE

(Red House 142)

Conclusion

There's an ocean of blues out there. We've only surveyed a few of its waters. Listen, explore, and you will find many more singers of yesterday and today who will impress and entertain you as much as the few we've been able to squeeze between these covers.

Though the sounds of blues have not changed as rapidly or as greatly through time over the past quarter century as they did before then, the fact that there are *so many* people singing and playing blues today (and more making blues recordings than there ever have been before, by far) means that you'll always have new voices and new songs to enjoy, along with all those treasures from the past. We do hope this book has enlightened your journey.

Discographical Note

More blues is available today than has ever been available before. The choices can be bewildering. Not every blues CD is pure gold; magnificent new music and reissues assembled with the greatest of care share the blues bins with schlocky products that only exist to snare a loose dollar or two.

Throughout this book we have recommended certain CDs. Most of them are domestic (American) releases. All are available in American stores (at least the more comprehensive big-city stores or online services) as of press time. Of course, new CDs are constantly being released, and old ones deleted from the catalog, so take our listings with a grain of salt.

For artists with large catalogues, we've tried to pick the CDs with the original versions of their best-known, most influential songs.

There's a trend toward releasing multiple-disc sets, or series of CDs, containing an artist's complete recorded works. This is nirvana for serious collectors; for the new bluesfan, buying a 3-CD set of an unfamiliar artist may be a rather daunting proposition. On the other hand, there are still certain artists (especially from the pre-WWII era) who are not well represented, or whose CDs are not generally available in the U.S.A. (that's why we list no CDs for Peetie Wheatstraw, for instance). If current trends hold, most of the ones covered in this book will show up sooner or later. All the major blues magazines regularly review new releases and re-releases; simply watch for your favorites.

A Selective Bibliography

Robert Johnson never saw his name in a book or magazine as long as he lived. Until the 1950s there was very little published writing of any kind about blues, aside from incidental mentions in jazz literature. Now we have a couple of shelves full of good books, and three thriving glossy magazines in the U.S.A. alone.

Brooks, Lonnie, Cub Koda and Wayne Baker Brooks: *Blues For Dummies*. This ubiquitous series of yellow paperbacks has covered everything from computers to beer, so why not blues? There's solid information here, along with plenty of diverting trivia and lots of those cute Dummies logos.

Calt, Stephen and Gayle Wardlow: *The Life and Music of Charlie Patton: King of the Delta Blues*. Newton, NJ: Rock Chapel Press, 1988. About as definitive a biography of this Delta pioneer as we're ever likely to see, exhaustively researched in Mississippi while many of Patton's contemporaries were still alive (1965-72).

Cohodas, Nadine: *Spinning Blues Into Gold: The Chess Brothers and the legendary Chess Records*. New York: St. Martin's Press, 2000. A thorough, exactingly researched but remarkably readable history of the most important record company of the post-WWII blues scene, the immigrant brothers who ran it, and the rough-and-tumble indie record business in general.

Cowley, John and Paul Oliver, ed.: *The New Blackwell Guide to Recorded Blues*. Oxford: Blackwell Publishers, 1996. Comprehensive reviews and track listings of some 560 blues CDs, together with introductory essays on various genres, by fourteen eminent blues scholars.

Dance, Helen Oakley: *Stormy Monday: The T-Bone Walker Story*. New York: Da Capo Press, 1987. The story of blues' first great electric guitarist, told largely in his own words and those of his friends and relatives.

Davis, Francis: *The History of the Blues*. New York: Hyperion, 1995. Though not a reference book as much as it is a fascinating, entertaining, convincing interpretation of the music, this does cover the whole story quite nicely.

Deffaa, Chip: *Blue Rhythms: Six Lives In Rhythm and Blues*. Urbana: University of Illinois Press, 1996. Revealing profiles of Ruth Brown, Little Jimmy Scott, Charles Brown, Floyd Dixon, LaVern Baker and Jimmy Witherspoon, based on the author's intensive interviews with the singers.

Edwards, David Honeyboy, as told to Janis Martinson and Michael Robert Frank: *The World Don't Owe Me Nothing: The Life and Times of Delta Bluesman Honeyboy Edwards*. Chicago: Chicago Review Press, 1997. Edwards may not be the Delta's greatest bluesman, but he was and is a good one. Now that he's outlived virtually all his contemporaries, his memories cast precious light on bygone days.

Ferris, William: *Blues From The Delta*. New York: Da Capo Press, 1978. The author spent a decade (1967-76) recording and interviewing active Mississippi bluesmen, originally for a Ph.D. dissertation. This book is a scholarly yet lively account of what he heard and learned.

Garon, Paul and Beth: *Woman With Guitar: Memphis Minnie's Blues*. New York: Da Capo Press, 1992. Thoroughly researched biography of this pioneer urban singer-guitarist, with intensive analyses of her lyrics and a lot of cogent theorizing about the significance of Minnie's music and blues in general.

Garon, Paul: *Blues and the Poetic Spirit*. New York: Da Capo Press, 1975. An intense, contentious analysis of the meaning of blues lyrics, primarily from the 1920s and 1930s but with some post-WWII examples as well. Portions of the book devoted to specific subject areas (drugs, weapons, "eros," etc.) are especially illuminating.

Gillett, Charlie: *The Sound Of The City: The Rise of Rock and Roll*. Revised edition. New York: Pantheon Books, 1983. The story of the independent record labels that first revitalized blues in the 1940s and early 1950s, and subsequently became prime outlets for rock 'n' roll. An update of a pioneering work first published in 1970.

Guralnick, Peter: *Searching For Robert Johnson*. New York: Dutton, 1989. In these 83 pages is most of what is known or suspected about the shadowy figure who's now the most celebrated of all pre-WWII bluesmen.

Harris, Sheldon: *Blues Who's Who*. New Rochelle, NY: Arlington House, 1979. What this huge book has: reams of well-researched data on every significant bluesman from the beginning to the 1970s, where they were born, what songs they recorded, the clubs they played at, etc. etc. plus hundreds of fine photos. What it doesn't have, by design: any attempt at critical assessment of the music. What it needs: an update.

Herzhaft, Gerard: *Encyclopedia of the Blues*. 2nd edition. Fayetteville: University of Arkansas Press, 1997. Though not as comprehensive or as well written as Robert Santelli's similar-sized *Big Book Of Blues* (q.v.), this volume does have some good insights and a nice alphabetical listing of standard blues songs.

King, B.B. with David Ritz: *Blues All Around Me: The Autobiography of B.B. King*. New York: Avon Books, 1996. The superstar's frank but graceful, eloquent and entertaining life story—with his revealing words on the music he loves, the people who've wounded and supported him, and plenty of war stories from his decades on the road (including a few X-rated ones).

Kostelanetz, Richard: *The B.B. King Companion*. New York: Schirmer Books, 1997. An anthology of articles about B.B., taken from newspapers, learned journals and everything in between, from 1952 to 1996. Includes numerous interviews with the man himself, and a very early magazine piece by the author of the book you're holding. Indexed.

Lemann, Nicholas: *The Promised Land: The Great Black Migration and How It Changed America*. New York: Alfred A. Knopf, 1991. A splendid treatise on the river of humanity that flowed from the rural South to the nation's cities in the 1940s, and profoundly affected the course of blues.

Lipscomb, Mance, as told to and compiled by Glen Alyn: *I Say Me For a Parable: The Oral Autobiography of Mance Lipscomb, Texas Bluesman*. New York: Da Capo Press, 1993. Songster Mance Lipscomb was also a great talker; here are his stories. His Texas drawl is phonetically reproduced throughout ("If you wanta know sumpn…") which can be disconcerting until you get used to it.

Lomax, Alan: *The Land Where the Blues Began*. New York: Pantheon Books, 1993. The man who "discovered" Lead Belly, Muddy Waters and hundreds of other singers assembles convincing theories about blues' early development, based on his extensive field recording experience in the U.S.A. and abroad, dating back to the 1930s.

Oakley, Giles: *The Devil's Music: A History Of the Blues*. New York: Da Capo Press, 1997. A general history of the music, originally published in 1976 to accompany a BBC documentary, and revised in 1983. With a 1997 afterword. Well-researched and comprehensive.

Oliver, Paul: *Blues Off The Record: Thirty Years of Blues Commentary*. New York: Da Capo Press, 1984. Illuminating essays on individual blues singers and general topics covering the acoustic and early electric eras. The British-born Oliver is the dean of active blues writers.

Palmer, Robert: *Deep Blues*. New York: Penguin Books, 1981. Palmer skillfully and entertainingly traces the history of Delta blues and its electric Chicago offspring, with in-depth studies of Muddy Waters, Sunnyland Slim, Sonny Boy Williamson (No. 2) and others.

Patoski, Joe Nick and Bill Crawford: *Stevie Ray Vaughan: Caught In the Crossfire*. Boston: Little, Brown, 1993. A carefully researched, well-written biography of the young Texan whose fiery music jump-started the contemporary blues revival.

Robertson, Brian: *Little Blues Book*. Chapel Hill: Algonquin Books, 1996. Brief quotations from blues lyrics, loosely arranged by subject matter, with illustrations reproduced from some "blues trading cards" designed in 1980 by the redoubtable R. Crumb., and some neat lists of blues trivia. The ultimate blues stocking-stuffer.

Rowe, Mike: *Chicago Blues*. New York: Da Capo, 1988. This book remains the definitive work on the glory days of the Chicago Electric scene. Many rare and marvelous photographs.

Santelli, Robert: *The Big Book Of Blues*. New York: Penguin Books, 1993. This "biographical encyclopedia" covers all kinds of blues artists. Though not quite defectless (Percy Mayfield was not Curtis Mayfield's father!), this is the most useful, reliable book of its kind available.

Shaw, Arnold: *Honkers and Shouters: The Golden Years of Rhythm and Blues*. New York: Collier Books, 1978. Fascinating, revealing profiles and anecdotes from the uproarious R&B record business of the 1940s and 1950s.

Southern, Eileen: *The Music of Black Americans*. 3rd ed. New York: W. W. Norton, 1997. A thorough but readable textbook which attempts to cover the entirety of African-American musical endeavors in the United States from the arrival of the first slaves to the 1990s, from slave songs to symphonies to rap. Treatment of blues and other 20th century forms is necessarily brief, but Southern's account of black music in earlier centuries provides invaluable background.

Tooze, Sandra: *Muddy Waters - The Mojo Man*. Toronto: ECW Press, 1997. A thorough but lively biography of the kingpin of the Electric Chicago scene. Includes excellent photos and an exhaustive discography.

Wilcock, Donald E. with Buddy Guy: *Damn Right I've Got the Blues: Buddy Guy and the Roots of Rock-and-Roll*. San Francisco: Woodford Press, 1993. An entertaining, revealing autobiography of the eminent electric guitarist, with numerous testimonials from rock stars inspired by his music.

Magazines

Living Blues was founded in Chicago in 1970, a year before Alligator Records. That period was just about the nadir of blues history, and the magazine's name had a defensive ring to it at the time. However, it has grown and prospered along with the revival, and is now part of a multifaced blues research and teaching organization based at the University of Mississippi. Its bimonthly pages include well-written profiles of active singers famous and obscure, news items, festival calendars, record reviews, and comprehensive obituaries, along with plenty of photos.

Living Blues is subtitled "The Magazine of the African-American Blues Tradition," and that's what it is: no feature articles on white artists are to be found in *Living Blues*, though white blues is covered in record reviews and other items.

After having the field to itself for two decades, *Living Blues* now has a pair of worthy competitors. *Blues Revue* comes out ten times a year; *Blues Access* is a quarterly. Aside from that they're fairly similar, both filled with lively features on current blues stars and up-and-comers along with news, record reviews, and a few items intended for budding musicians. Both also do a few historical pieces, and yes, both do cover white blues artists extensively.

There are also local blues periodicals in various American cities; look for these at clubs and record stores.

Living Blues, Center for the Study of Southern Culture, The University of Mississippi, University, MS 38677-9836.

Blues Access, 1455 Chestnut Pl., Boulder, CO 80304.

Blues Revue, Straight-Up Corp., Rt. 2, Box 118, West Union, WV 26456-9520.

Blues Online

Blues may be lovably low-tech music that takes great pride in its ties to the past…but it has an abundant presence on that great icon of the future, the Internet. Many contemporary artists have their own websites…and many who died long before the Internet was ever dreamed of have websites too, thanks to loyal fans.

You can find a whole lot of nuggets simply by opening your favorite search engine and entering the name of an artist who interests you. Here are a few sites of general interest:

BluesNet: http://www.hub.org/bluesnet/

University of Mississippi Libraries Blues Archive: http://sunset.backbone.olemiss.edu/depts/general_library/files/bluesarc.htm

Bluesworld: www.bluesworld.com

Yahoo Entertainment—Blues: http://www.yahoo.com/entertainment/music/artists/By_Genre/Blues

BLUES VENUES— A Random Sampling

Muddy Waters' juke house, Mississippi, ca. 1940
"Muddy Waters' juke house was in full swing. The home-made whiskey was selling briskly, fish were frying in the kitchen, and under the flickering light of coal oil lamps, knots of men were throwing dice, squinting intently to make out the numbers that came up. Muddy was playing the blues…"
—*Robert Palmer, Deep Blues, p. 95*

Florence's, Chicago (South Side), ca. 1970
"Six days a week, Florence's was just another anonymous tavern in the heart of the city's black community. But every Sunday afternoon… Florence's rocked to the music of Hound Dog Taylor and the HouseRockers. Blues musicians from all over the city and all over the world dropped by to jam and party with some of Chicago's staunchest (and hardest-drinking) blues fans. Just to get into Florence's, you had to circle around the pig ear sandwich truck parked in front, pass the sidewalk dice game, and slip through the clump of men outside the door drinking from brown paper bags. Once you got in, it was hard to see the band over the crowd. Florence's wasn't even big enough to have a bandstand. They just moved a few tables out from the back of the club, the band rolled in their

amps, and folks danced in the narrow aisle between the bar and the rickety booths."
—*Bruce Iglauer, notes to The Alligator Records 20th Anniversary Collection*

Antone's, Austin, ca. 1976
The element of danger that permeated Sixth Street made it all the more exciting. When Boz Scaggs, the Dallas native who made it big in San Francisco as a white soul artist, brought an entourage to hear Bobby Bland one night, that mystique was further embellished. Scaggs wanted to see Bland during a break and pushed past a security guard to get backstage. Perhaps he did not hear the guard inform him that Bland was busy changing outfits. Maybe he didn't want to hear him. Whatever the circumstances, rules were rules, even for uppity rock stars. The guard decked Scaggs with a single punch, and removed his person to the sidewalk by the backstage door.

A Blues Glossary

barrelhouse, n. 1) An inelegant drinking establishment of the Prohibition era or earlier, generally with musical entertainment. —, adj. Characteristic of the music performed in such establishments. —, v. = BOOGIE.

boogie, n. A fast blues. —, v. 1) To dance to a fast blues. 2) To celebrate together, often with music and with alcohol or other drugs; to "party" in the modern sense of that word. 3) To have sex.

bottleneck, n. 1) A neck from a bottle, or other device of similar shape, used as a slide in guitar playing. —, adj. Played with a bottleneck.

doctor, n. 1) A practitioner of medicine, including folk medicine. 2) A practitioner of magic; one who prepares charms and casts spells, often in ways related to practices of *voudon* (voodoo).

drylongso, adj. Not good.

eagle flies on Friday, the. I get my paycheck on Friday.

fo' day creep. "Before-day creep"—i.e. a

BLUES RESOURCES

surreptitious night-time visit for purposes of extra-marital sex. Sometimes mis-transcribed as "four day creep."

gospel, or **gospel music**, n. 1) An African-American variety of religious music, utilizing primarily songs composed since the 1930s, and often featuring lead vocals that increase in intensity throughout the performance. Melismas (q.v.) are characteristic of gospel vocals. 2) African-American religious music in general.

harp, n. A harmonica.

hoodoo, n. A charm or spell intended to bring harm to someone. —, v. To cast a spell intended to bring harm to someone. **hoodoo man**, n. One who casts hoodoos.

jook joint (or **juke joint** or **juke house**), n. 1) A rural home or outbuilding used as a drinking establishment, with musical entertainment. 2) Any small establishment where R&B can be heard. Related to **jukebox**.

melisma, n. A group of several notes sung to a single syllable of lyrics.

mojo, n. A good luck charm, often purchased from a "doctor" (q.v., sense 2). "They were little red flannel bags that smelled of oils and perfumes; some were pierced by a needle or two." (Palmer, *Deep Blues*, p. 95-6).

R&B, n. Abbreviation of "rhythm and blues."

rhythm and blues, n. 1) Contemporary secular music recorded and purchased on records primarily by African Americans—a term coined by the trade magazine *Billboard* in 1948. 2) Popular African-American music of the late 1950s and early 1960s, including electric blues, doo-wop and soul. Note: *Billboard* recently returned to using this term as it did in 1948, to refer to today's contemporary African-American music. Many other writers continue to use sense (2).

sharecropping, n. A system of tenant farming in which landlords receive a portion of the farm's proceeds in lieu of rent.

soul, or **soul music**, n. A variety of R&B featuring gospel-style singing, and harmonic structures based on gospel music and/or mid-20th-century pop music.

zydeco, n. A blend of Cajun music and R&B, chiefly identified with Clifton Chenier (1925-1987).

RHINO RECORDS
has released an anthology of CDs called Blues Masters.

BLUES MASTERS, VOLUME 1: URBAN BLUES (Rhino 71121)

BLUES MASTERS, VOLUME 2: POSTWAR CLASSICS (Rhino 71122)

BLUES MASTERS, VOLUME 3: TEXAS BLUES (Rhino 71123)

BLUES MASTERS, VOLUME 4: HARMONICA CLASSICS (Rhino 71124)

BLUES MASTERS, VOLUME 5: JUMP BLUES CLASSICS (Rhino 71125)

BLUES MASTERS, VOLUME 6: BLUES ORIGINALS (Rhino 71127)

BLUES MASTERS, VOLUME 7: BLUES REVIVAL (Rhino 71128)

BLUES MASTERS, VOLUME 8: MISSISSIPPI DELTA BLUES (Rhino 71130)

BLUES MASTERS, VOLUME 9: POSTMODERN BLUES (Rhino 71132)

BLUES MASTERS, VOLUME 10: BLUES ROOTS (Rhino 71135)

BLUES MASTERS, VOLUME 11: CLASSIC BLUES WOMEN (Rhino 71134)

BLUES MASTERS, VOLUME 12: MEMPHIS BLUES (Rhino 71129)

BLUES MASTERS, VOLUME 13: NEW YORK CITY BLUES (Rhino 71131)

BLUES MASTERS, VOLUME 14: MORE JUMP BLUES (Rhino 71133)

BLUES MASTERS, VOLUME 15: SLIDE GUITAR CLASSICS (Rhino 71126)